Praise for
The Essential Handbook For Selling a Home

"This book is extremely helpful! The writing flows so well that I felt like Karen was right there coaching me through the entire process."

Courtney Peterson

"Karen Rittenhouse has done it again! Her first book encompassed everything you ever wanted to know about buying a house and this one, *The Essential Handbook For Selling a Home*, is exactly what home owners need to read as we continue to be in such an unpredictable selling market. This is something I will be giving my Sellers on all my listing appointments!"

Kathy Haines
Broker-in-Charge, All Property Solutions

"Reading Karen Rittenhouse's first book, *The Essential Handbook for Buying a Home* was an easy read, almost conversational. With this her second book, Karen guides the reader down the path of selling a home. It will serve as an easy to use reference whether you're selling a home now or planning to do so in the future. Sit back, relax, enjoy the read and listen to what Karen has to share about selling a home."

Dave Kiddy
Investor and President of Triad Real Estate Investors Association

"The wealth of information conveyed so concisely in every book written by Karen makes her books a reference that I can pull from my shelf every time I need to buy or sell a home. Each of us can learn from Karen's experience and knowledge and avoid making mistakes that can cost thousands in our own pockets."

Debbie Brower
CPA

"I have worked with Karen Rittenhouse for many years. She has a passion and a goal to share her knowledge in buying and selling real estate. She has been a top performer in all her endeavors and a mentor to many in the real estate business. Her success story is one to follow. Her personal experience in real estate has given her the ability to walk you through the process of buying or selling a home without being overwhelmed by the uncertainties of the experience. I value her expertise as a friend and a mentor."

Terry Parker
Real Estate Investor

The Essential Handbook
for Selling a Home

The Essential Handbook

FOR SELLING A HOME

Karen Rittenhouse

Southeastern Investments, LLC
Greensboro, North Carolina

Published by Southeastern Investments, LLC
Greensboro, North Carolina

ISBN 13: 978-0-9837752-0-1
Library of Congress Control Number: 2012900266

First Southeastern Investments, LLC printing: January 2012

Dedication

To all those struggling to sell their home in a buyer's market!

"In the middle of every difficulty lies opportunity."

Albert Einstein

Contents

Acknowledgements

Thank you to so many of my friends and family for helping me with this book. I want to especially thank Scott Shubert, mortgage loan originator with Benchmark Mortgage for his help with all things mortgage.

I also thank my favorite Realtors, Kathy Haines of All Property Solutions and Pam Wilson of Home Selling Solutions for their input and suggestions.

And thanks, as always, to my boys—John, Glenn, and Jim—for their continued support and encouragement. Real estate has been very, very good to us!

Introduction

Why read this book?

Why should you read this book? Because selling a home will be easier when you're prepared! And, buyers should be lined up at your door with offers in hand!

As you read, I'm going to answer some of your basic questions including: How do I market my house? How do I know what it's worth? Should I list with a real estate agent? How do I prepare the house for sale? How do I know if a buyer is qualified? How long will this process take?

You'll discover how easy it is to prepare your property for sale, determine the value of your property, understand multiple selling strategies, and be confident, when you sell, that you received a fair price for you home.

I've been involved in real estate full-time since January 2005. I love real estate. After buying and selling over 150 homes and coaching others to do the same, I've found that most home sellers have the same questions and concerns. I help buyers and sellers every month and, in this book, I am going to share some of the most frequently discussed questions and answers for people, just like you, who are selling single family homes.

People sell houses every day, but you probably don't. The more informed you are going in, the more confident you will be, the easier the process, and the better your chance of making a good deal, maybe even a great deal, when you sell.

What's inside?

For ease of use, this book is divided into sections allowing you to read from beginning to end or to jump around easily to specific topics.

I start with *Section 1: The Decision*. Should you even sell your home? Is it a good time? Is it better to keep it and rent it out?

Then *Section 2: Selling Options* explores some of the choices you may be familiar with but not really understand, such as owner financing and selling through auction.

Next is *Section 3: Preparing to Sell,* where we discuss getting your documents in order, and preparing your home for market, including rehabbing and landscaping tips.

Section 4: Marketing covers how to determine the value of your home, how to effectively market the property, and what you need to know about having an open house.

In *Section 5: The Process*, you will learn so much including negotiating offers, home inspections, appraisals, and what you could pay in closing costs.

Section 6: Sold! sums it all up with the physical part—your moving process. We also discuss the risks of leaving your home vacant if you need to move before it sells.

Being able to talk the talk

If this is your first time selling a home, you may feel over-whelmed. Don't panic! We discuss the process in easy to understand terms. Once you understand some basic vocabulary, your fear will melt away. In no time, you'll be comfortable using all the vocabulary necessary for getting your home sold.

For your convenience, a glossary of frequently used terms appears at the end of this book providing quick and easy reference.

Section One

THE
DECISION

L et's begin with your ultimate decision: Is this a good
time to sell? Throughout this book, I've made the
assumption that you've already decided to sell, hence
the book title. However, you may not be quite clear yet
about whether selling now is the right thing to do.

To give some clarity, I'm going to cover:

- Understanding your local economy

- Why there aren't qualified buyers

- Whether or not this is a good time to sell

Chapter 1

ARE WE AT THE BOTTOM OF THE REAL ESTATE MARKET?

A re we at the bottom of the real estate market? And how do we determine "at" or "near" the bottom?

The answer, as always, depends upon your local economic and housing market conditions. Real estate is always local. To research and learn your local area, check out newspapers, online news services, and industry websites for a wealth of data that can be used to analyze your local market trends. CNN is not local.

The current real estate economy

To begin let's discuss, briefly, what's been happening in the U.S. housing market.

House values can be tracked historically. Typically, values rise and fall in a pretty well-defined seven-to-nine-year cycle up, followed by seven to nine years down. This cycle has been fairly

Some predict we will not see another significant increase in real estate values in our lifetimes.

reliable since the Great Depression when records began being kept. More recently, the real estate market was at a low in 1985 and climbed back up until about 1992.

Housing then declined until 1999 when the market turned again, and prices increased until about 2006. At that point, we experienced real estate euphoria where everyone could get a loan. In fact, as we've come to learn, many people who should never have gotten loans got them.

To entice people who weren't able to afford large house payments, lenders gave borrowers adjustable rate mortgages (ARMs). These loans started with very low interest rates, enabling the buyer to afford the monthly payments, but adjusted to higher rates over time, levels they should have been to begin with. Buyers were told, "When your rates adjust up, simply refinance to new, lower rates or put more money down so you owe less."

Sounded great. However, at the same time these interest rates were adjusting up, house prices actually declined, so borrowers did not qualify for refinances. Borrowers could not afford the adjusted higher monthly payments and began to default on loans in record numbers. The market flooded with foreclosures driving prices down even further and, ultimately, the bubble burst.

So, is the seven-year down cycle 2006 to 2013? We'll see. We may not be at the absolute bottom of this most recent cycle, but we're certainly bouncing at or near the bottom. How long we remain here is uncertain.

Some predict we will not see another significant increase in real estate values in our lifetimes. That does not, however, fit the historical model. Housing prices have always rebounded after a period of decline. Add to that the projected population growth, and it becomes likely we'll see an increased need for newer and additional housing.

When trying to understand your local real estate market, there are some basic factors you should pay attention to.

Five indicators to consider:

1. **Number of homes for sale.** A large inventory of homes for sale typically indicates a weak housing market which indicates lower housing prices. If your area has an inventory of twelve months, that means it would take one year for all the homes currently on the market to be sold. And remember, new homes are being listed all the time, especially in the spring. High inventory forces sellers to lower prices to compete for qualified buyers.

   The U.S. population is projected to increase by 49 million between 2010 and 2030.

2. **How long have they been on the market?** In a fast-paced market, homes sell quickly and this causes prices to rise. On the other hand, homes that sit on the market for weeks or months lead sellers to lower prices causing pricing, and values, to decline. Ultimately, the value of your home is based upon what someone will pay to buy it.

3. **How many have sold?** Faster sales suggest a stronger market, and greater desire/demand leads to higher prices.

4. **Are builders offering concessions?** Builders offer discounts, free upgrades, and gifts when the market is weak. A lack of these incentives suggests builders have limited inventory. Lack of builder inventory reduces the number of available homes and contributes to stable pricing.

5. **Are rents rising?** Rising rents indicates more tenants and fewer rental vacancies. With many people losing homes to foreclosure and short sales and damaging their credit, the

number of tenants is increasing, vacancies are decreasing, and rents are on the rise. More people turning to rentals indicates fewer available buyers.

> *Ultimately, the value of your home is based upon what someone will pay to buy it.*

Cost vs. value

In the current real estate market, properties are being sold at great discounts. There is always the chance that prices may fall further, forcing you, the seller, to lower prices even more in the future. How do you know? How long can you wait in the hope that the real estate market will improve? If you wait, can you risk that values may drop even further?

But, value isn't always about financial cost. Rather than considering market conditions only, it may be better to simply consider the needs of your family. Is it worth it to take less for your home today if it allows you and your family to move on to the next better house, job, school, or location?

> *Take comfort in knowing that, when you buy, you will make up for any loss you may take when you sell.*

And recognize that, even if you are forced to lower your price below what you want to get for your home, you will also be buying your next home at these same great discounts. Take comfort in knowing that, when you buy, you will make up for any loss you may take when you sell.

Chapter 2

THIS MARKET IS TOUGH

elling can be hard—really hard. It's a "buyer's market" because so many for-sale homes are available. Because of the number of available homes on the market, house prices are depressed. What does this mean to you? You'll have to price your home below what the market says it's worth to attract the few qualified, interested buyers. You have to put upgrade money into a property just to prepare it to sell at a discounted price.

This is a really tough time to sell a house. Why?

- There are a ton of homes on the market, meaning you have lots of competition for qualified buyers.

- Buyers want foreclosure prices even if your home is in perfect condition.

■ Buyers have so much to choose from that they want all the bells and whistles—hard surface countertops, hardwood floors, fireplace, deck, fenced yard, fresh paint, new carpets.

■ And, again, they want foreclosure prices!

■ Selling is expensive! You have to discount to compete, then there's real estate commission, closing costs, survey, inspection, repairs after it's been inspected, current year property taxes, attorney costs, recording fees—where's the profit?

Add to that the national decline in housing values. Because of the decline, you could be "upside down" on your mortgage (meaning you owe more than your house is worth). You may have to sell your home for less than you owe, meaning you have to write a check at the closing table just to get rid of it.

There aren't many qualified buyers. Why?

Because it's so hard to qualify! Lenders are looking for high credit scores, large down payments—many require 20 percent—low debt-to-income ratios, and significant cash reserves in the buyer's bank account.

And, it's not just the buyer under tougher scrutiny, but the property as well. Lenders are tough on inspectors and even sellers. Lenders want more repairs done prior to closing than in the past and fewer credits given from sellers to buyers at closing for future repairs.

What's the good news?

The good news is that houses are selling, and they always do. There are qualified buyers out there and homes are being sold every day. You have to make sure these buyers see yours and, ultimately, pick yours.

Selling your home is no time for ego. This is a purely business transaction. To you it's a home filled with memories and your

> *Selling your home is no time for ego. This is a purely business transaction.*

personal touches; to prospective buyers it's a house. Give them reason to make it their home.

And, again, even though you're selling for less, you'll be buying for less once you sell.

What can you do to compete? Don't worry; I'm going to cover that in the upcoming sections.

Chapter 3

RENT YOUR HOME OR SELL IT?

H ave you considered renting out your home? Even if you think there is no way you ever would, don't discard this chapter. There maybe valuable information here you haven't considered.

With all the foreclosed properties available today, you'll have a lot of competition for the few buyers who can qualify. And, thanks to all the newscasts, people expect to find great deals from banks (real estate owned - REOs), as well as from individual sellers.

Rather than losing your home to foreclosure or selling at a huge discount, you may want to consider renting your home in this growing renter's market. As fewer qualified buyers are looking at more homes than ever on the market, your options may be leading you to this solution.

If you need to sell quickly and the odds are your house will sit for a while, how about renting it out?

Rent your home or sell it?

According to census data analyzed by Harvard's Joint Center for Housing Studies and The Associated Press, the number of single-family rentals nationwide jumped 2.3 million from 2006

Rather than losing your home to foreclosure or selling at a huge discount, you may want to consider renting your home in this growing renter's market.

to 2010. During the first half of the decade, it increased only 720,000.

Since the housing meltdown, nearly 3 million households have become renters. At least 3 million more are expected by 2015. Rentals are on the rise!

Homeownership is at its lowest point since 1998 and has declined for six straight years.

Let's look at some pros and cons of renting versus selling.

RENTING PROS

- Renting your home prevents selling now at a loss or losing your home to foreclosure.

- Renting your home "should" cover your costs of ownership (or nearly cover them) so you can move on without the concern of that overhead.

- Renting, over time, should create an income stream for you and your family.

- Someone else is paying down your mortgage.

- Renting will give you added tax deductions.

- The property will provide income over time and for your retirement.

- We're in a buyer's market, meaning there are more homes for sale than there are buyers to buy.

- Fewer people are able to qualify for a home loan because borrowing requirements have tightened, meaning even if someone wants to buy your home, they may not be able to.

- The number of people preferring to rent homes is increasing.

RENTING CONS

- Dealing with tenants. (which can be handled by a property management company)

- Tenants could damage your property. (We hear this concern a lot but, fortunately, it never deterred us. In actuality, 95 percent of all tenant "damage" is normal wear and tear and the costs to maintain a rental property are, over time, much lower than the value gained.)

- If you continue to try to sell your home while tenant occupied, it could create challenges.

- It may be more difficult to rent out if potential tenants know that potential buyers will be walking through and the house could be sold out from under them at any moment.

> *In actuality, 95 percent of all tenant "damage" is normal wear and tear and the costs to maintain a rental property are, over time, much lower than the value gained.*

SELLING PROS

- The money you make from the sale can be applied to the new purchase.

- No tenants.

SELLING CONS

- You may have to sell at a significantly reduced price, even a loss.

- No potential gain in value when the market turns around.

- No opportunity for income or to have a tenant pay down your loan balance.

- You may experience tax consequences on any profits.

I recommend holding property as a rental to anyone who is willing. If you rent your home out, the property should create cash flow, meaning it brings in more every month than it costs for your mortgage, taxes, and insurance. Even if it doesn't cover 100 percent of your expenses, you may be able to rent your home out for enough to allow you and your family to move on now.

No matter how much rent you receive, it will cost you to keep the property. Vacancies, damage, and upkeep are inevitable. We find, however, that over time, value gained through holding our properties far, far, far outweighs the expense and aggravation to maintain them.

If you can't sell your home for what you need to pay off your debt, consider renting it out until you can make a profit on it in the future.

Property management

If you decide to rent out your home and manage it yourself, your rental should be handled by you as a business, even if you have only one property. Don't become emotionally involved with your tenants. Have rules and stick to them. If well managed, it will prosper. If poorly managed, it will fail.

Should you decide to rent out your home but do not want to deal with tenants on your own, contact local property management companies for assistance. When hiring a property management company, be aware that:

- There are management companies who won't be as concerned with selecting good tenants and maintaining the property as you would.

- You don't want just anyone to manage the property; you'll want a reputable company to handle it for you.

- You'll need to interview multiple management companies and check references and referrals until you find one that you trust.

- Management fees will take part of your profits. These fees can make the difference between positive cash flow (money left over after all expenses) and negative cash flow. Be sure you know your true numbers before making a decision.

- The management company you hire should go over your numbers with you and give you a realistic idea of your costs and potential income.

If you can't sell your home now for what you need to pay off your debt, consider renting it out until you can make a profit on it in the future.

Section Two

SELLING OPTIONS

There are many ways to sell a home other than the traditional put-a-for-sale-sign-in-the-yard-and-have-a-buyer-get-a-bank-loan. Here are some you may have heard about but may not understand:

- Short sale

- Auction

- Owner financing

- Lease option

- The "what if" of foreclosure

The main point of this section is to be sure you know that *you do* have selling options.

Chapter 4

SHORT SALE

Are you "upside down" on your mortgage? Do you owe more to the lender than what your house is worth? Is this what is keeping you from being able to sell your home?

Or, perhaps you and/or your spouse have lost jobs due to downsizing or health issues. An alternative may be to talk with your lender about a short sale. Before you do anything, however, know as much as you can going in.

What is a short sale?

A short sale is when a mortgage is sold *short* of what is owed. As a result of this type of transaction, the bank takes a loss. For example, if you owe $200,000, your lender may agree to let you sell the property for only $150,000 and be willing to forgive the difference. In some cases, because you can market it for less than its value, this would allow you to sell your property quickly.

> *In some cases, because you can market it for less than its value, a short sale would allow you to sell your property quickly.*

The lender accepts the less-than-full repayment of the mortgage in order to avoid what would amount to a larger loss for them if they were to foreclose. Because the lender receives less than the actual loan balance, the seller receives nothing from a short sale.

Contrary to popular belief, a seller does not have to be behind on their mortgage to request a short sale; they simply have to show that the house cannot be sold for what is owed. The lender agrees to *write-off* as much of the mortgage as is needed for the home to be sold at current market value.

When a loan is "shorted" and the lender accepts less than the full amount as a pay off, they will often go after the seller for the unpaid balance by placing a deficiency judgment against the seller. It is possible for sellers to be released by the lender from their obligation to repay the shorted amount, or deficiency, but not all lenders will do this. Release from obligation to repay is a negotiating process that should be included when working a short sale.

Will a short sale hurt your credit?

If the lender considers this transaction paid satisfactorily, it won't hurt your credit score. However, if the lender reports this sale as "settled for less than the full amount due," it will negatively impact your score. Be sure to check with your lender before you enter into a short sale to find out how they report "shorts" to the credit bureaus.

Another possible impact is that the IRS views unpaid debt as income and will tax you on the forgiven amount.

Short sales can absolutely help you out of a bad situation; just know the

Contrary to popular belief, a seller does not have to be behind on their mortgage to request a short sale; the seller simply has to show that the house cannot be sold for what is owed.

facts before you enter any transaction and determine if it's the best solution for you.

What is a deficiency judgment?

Deficiency judgment is a judgment in favor of the lender and against the seller for the remainder of the debt not completely cleared by the sale of the property. As discussed in the short sale definition, the lender has allowed the seller to sell the property for less than the balance owed on the mortgage.

A deficiency judgment occurs when the lender does not, however, release the borrower from their personal obligation to repay the full amount that was owed before the short

The borrower may remain liable for the full amount of the remaining loan balance even if the property is sold for less.

sale occurred. In this instance, the borrower remains liable for the full amount of the remaining loan balance even if the property is sold for less. The seller/borrower must pay the difference between what the buyer pays for the property and the remaining loan balance.

Not all lenders place a deficiency judgment against the seller. Some lenders accept the amount of the short sale and "forgive" the remaining balance, allowing the seller to walk away cleared of all obligation for the balance of the loan that was unpaid. This forgiveness must be negotiated with the lender as part of the short sale agreement and not brought up after the deal has been completed.

Why would a mortgage lender accept a short sale rather than foreclose?

- Foreclosure processes and laws differ from state to state. Many lenders don't want to tie up their time, money, and legal resources trying to keep up with all the state-specific laws.

- The foreclosure process is time intensive and costly. Often, banks would rather cut their losses and work to replace these bad loans with good ones.

- The amount they have to hold in reserves is in direct relation to the amount of money they have tied up in REO properties. A little-known fact is that the lender must put aside eight times the amount of the loan in reserves. For example, if the bank owns a property for $100,000, they cannot lend out $800,000 because of that debt. For this reason, banks need to get foreclosures off their books.

Some lenders accept the amount of the short sale and "forgive" the remaining balance, allowing the seller to walk away cleared of all obligation for the balance of the loan that was unpaid.

For a property to qualify as a short sale

If you owe more than your home is worth and are considering a short sale, here are some of the more "typical" reasons a bank will accept one.

1. The home's true market value has dropped.

    Comparable area sales must show that the home is worth less than the unpaid balance still owed to the lender.

2. The mortgage is in or soon will be in default.

    It used to be that lenders would not consider a short sale if the payments were current. Now, in certain instances, they will work with the borrower before they are behind.

3. The seller has fallen on hard times.

    The seller must submit a "hardship letter" to the lender explaining why he or she cannot pay the amount due. The seller must show why he or she has stopped or will stop making payments.

    Examples of accepted hardships are:

    - Unemployment
    - Divorce
    - Medical emergency or sudden illness
    - Bankruptcy
    - Death

If the lender discovers any assets belonging to the seller, they may determine that the seller has the ability to repay the loan and, therefore, reject the short sale. Sellers with assets may be granted a short sale but could be required to pay back the balance (see deficiency judgment). The lender might, however, discount the amount the seller is required to pay back rather than requiring the full balance.

The lender might discount the amount the seller is required to pay back rather than requiring the full balance.

Is a short sale a good idea for your buyer?

- Short sales take a very long time (in most cases three to eight months minimum). If the buyer makes an offer on a short sale and neighborhood values continue to drop, by the time the bank makes a decision, their offer could be higher than the value of the property. In addition, while waiting on a short sale, your buyer might miss a better deal that comes along.

- Rather than accept their offer, the bank may make a counter offer or reject the offer completely, even after waiting months for their response. Short sales are not easy or fast.

- Typically, offers are submitted to the lender's short sale committee. Its decision can take as long as two to three months. Because it can take so long, most offers are contingent upon the lender responding within a certain time frame after which the buyer is free to cancel the offer.

Is a short sale a good idea for you?

- A short sale will show up on your credit report, typically dropping your score seventy-five to 100 points. Damage to the seller's credit is often considered not as bad as a foreclosure; however, many creditors make no distinction.

A short sale will show up on your credit report, typically dropping your score seventy-five to 100 points.

- Your lender will ultimately decide whether or not any offer is accepted; however, you also have the right to reject any offer you feel is too low. Remember, you may be responsible for any unpaid balance. Even if you accept the offer, there is no deal until the lender accepts it.

- Once an offer is accepted, you or your real estate agent submit the offer to the lender with the buyer's earnest money deposit. The lender will want to see that the buyer has been pre-approved for a loan, so be sure to submit their pre-approval letter with the offer. The agent should also submit a list of comparable area sales to support the sales price in the offer. Anything you and your agent can do to speed up the process is helpful.

> *Allow a minimum of sixty to ninety days for the short sale process to unfold.*

- Most short sales are sold "as is" because you, the seller, and the lender are losing money.

- Short sales are not fast or easy. Allow a minimum of sixty to ninety days for the short sale process. Once the lender accepts the offer, they will want to close within thirty days.

A short sale may work for you and may end up being your best solution. The important thing is to understand the process before you make the decision and to be sure to negotiate with your lender, before entering the process, forgiveness for the balance. Knowing ahead of time whether or not the lender will come after you for any "shorted" amount may help make that decision for you.

Chapter 5

SELLING YOUR PROPERTY THROUGH AUCTION

Need to get rid of your property in a hurry? The goal of an auction is to sell for a price you want on the day of your choice.

Benefits of selling through auction

Auctions are known to be fast and relatively easy. Typically, there are limited opportunities for potential buyers to view the property, often just a couple of hours before the sale, so sellers aren't inconvenienced by potential buyers trooping through the house for weeks or months. The sale itself is completed in a matter of minutes and closing takes place within thirty to forty-five days.

Property condition, naturally, may affect the final price, but you don't have to spend a lot on fix-up or paint. Buyers bid at their own risk. Auction properties come with no contingencies and no guarantees about the condition of the property. The standard language states: Properties are auctioned "where is, as is."

Oftentimes, selling prices are driven up by eager purchasers bidding against each other. We have gone to many house auctions only to be amazed that they, in our experience, typically sell for retail or even more than we think they're worth.

And, you have the benefit of knowing that, as soon as the bid is accepted, you have a legally binding contract. The purchaser pays a 10 percent deposit there and then and, in most states, must come up with the balance within thirty days. This avoids the uncertainty associated with selling a property in the conventional manner.

Finding an auctioneer

You can find auctioneers through the National Auctioneers Association (NAA), which includes an auction multiple listing service as well as an auctioneer search engine. Or, search your local newspaper for auction firms that do the most business in your area.

Choosing the right auctioneer is the first and most important step. Auctioneers specialize. Obviously, you want an auctioneer who specializes in your property type and location. Hiring an auctioneer who routinely handles sales of houses similar to yours will make them more likely to attract a crowd of buyers wanting a property like yours.

I recommend you make sure the auctioneer is licensed and a member of local as well as national associations so you can check credentials.

How the auctioneer is paid

Discuss with your auctioneer all the costs that will be associated with the sale. Some auctioneers charge a flat fee, most charge a percentage of the sales prices (about ten percent).

Know what they charge, how and when it's paid. Know if both you and the buyer pay a portion or if it will be charged to you as the seller. Also, can the marketing fees be added to the price you ask for the property? Know what the auction will cost so you can determine your minimum selling price.

Also important: If you change your mind or your reserve price is not met, how much will you still owe to the auctioneer?

Sell with reserve

If you decide to sell your property at auction, you'll want to "sell with reserve." This means there is a

An "absolute auction" is one where the property is sold to the highest bidder no matter what the price.

minimum price that must be met before you will approve the sale. An "absolute auction," on the other hand, is when the property is sold to the highest bidder no matter what the price. If only one bidder shows up and they bid $25 at an absolute auction, that's the sales price!

Preparation

Know the value of your property. If it sells for your asking price, you want to be sure it will appraise for at least that amount so your buyer is able to procure a large enough loan.

Some buyers will bring an inspector before they bid. It's best to get an inspection ahead of time so you and any potential buyers know what a buyer's inspector will find. If the buyer is purchasing with cash, you can sell "as is." If, however, they need to get a loan, banks are reluctant to loan on a property "as is." They want to know what they're lending against.

At the property on the day of the auction:

If using an auction company, some of these items will need to be provided by you; some they will provide.

1. Sign-in sheets

2. Flyers with property photos and information

3. Printed rules for the auction

4. Copy of the appraisal for buyers to view

5. Copy of the inspection for buyers to view

6. Copy of termite report, survey or any other reports you have for buyers to view

7. Bid sheets

Everyone must sign in. Get names and contact information. Allow them to browse the property at their convenience and ask questions.

If they want to bid, make sure they receive a packet of property information and that they place their bid on the bid sheet.

The best way to learn about auctions and decide if they might be the way to get your house sold is to attend some.

That evening, if handling the auction on your own, call the winning bidder to let them know they won the bid, or contact the top bidders and allow them to increase their bids until you determine a winning bidder. Sign a Purchase and Sale Agreement with the winner and let the next two people in line know that you will inform them if the sale does not go through.

If the sale is being handled by an auctioneer, the sale is final when your reserve price has been met or exceeded and the gavel drops.

Contact the mortgage lender and closing attorney and **stay on top of everything** until this sale closes!

If your property fails to meet its reserve:

That doesn't necessarily mean it's over. If you are willing to sell for less than the reserve, it's still possible to negotiate and do a deal with any of the bidders. The auction terms and conditions still remain, but as long as a price is agreed upon, the deal can go ahead.

Going, going, sold!

The best way to learn about auctions and decide if they might be the way to get your house sold is to attend some. Go to auctions to see what goes on, how it's done, and what kind of prices they bring.

If you decide that the high-pressure, fast-paced world of auctions is right for you, get prepared, get going, and get it sold!

Chapter 6

OWNER FINANCING

To sell your house quickly, offering flexible terms will increase your pool of interested buyers and thus the demand for your house. When selling your house the traditional way (you ask retail and the buyer borrows the purchase amount from a lender), you limit the number of prospective buyers and haven't done anything to stand out in the crowd.

Consider this: Suppose someone makes you a full price offer but they're not able to get the bank financing they need to close. Would you be willing or able to offer owner financing?

What exactly is owner financing, how does it work, and is it an advantage to you and the buyer?

What is owner financing?

With owner financing, the seller finances the property directly to the buyer. The seller acts as the bank and lends the purchaser all or part of the money needed to purchase the property. This is a great option when the prospective buyer cannot obtain funding through a conventional mortgage lender.

Suppose the buyer is able to get a loan for only a portion of the purchase price. Could you finance the balance? You would then have a second or "junior" lien against the property and their bank loan would make up the difference.

> *With owner financing, the seller acts as the bank and lends the purchaser all or part of the money needed to purchase the property.*

Owner finance examples

1. Let's begin with the simplest example, a property free and clear of any mortgage, with no debt on it. In this example, the buyer is paying $100,000 for your property. You receive 5 percent, $5000, in cash for the down payment. The buyer then signs a promissory note to you (an I.O.U.) promising to pay the additional $95,000. You sign and deliver a deed of ownership of the property to the buyer. The $95,000 promissory note is secured by the property and recorded as a lien against the property in favor of you. In this case, just like a traditional mortgage, you are acting as a lender to fund the purchase price of the house. Regular payments on the note are paid to you as agreed (in the terms spelled out in the note) until paid in-full.

   This is the same process a mortgage lender or bank goes through when lending a large sum using a house as collateral. All of this will be done, handled, and recorded by an attorney.

   You can extend the promissory note for any length of time you choose. It can be a fifteen-year or thirty-year note, just like a bank loan. Or, you can set a "balloon payment," a date by which the loan has to be paid in full. For example, you can allow the buyer to make payments over a period of five years, at which time the remaining balance is due in full. At that time, the buyer must either sell the property or get a new loan from a traditional bank or mortgage lender to pay you off. Your promissory note is then paid in full and your mortgage lien is removed from the property.

In this example, you were lending the entire amount to your buyer.

2. Now, for example two, suppose your buyer agrees to your $100,000 asking price has $10,000 to put down but only qualifies to borrow $80,000 from a lender. You could (a) turn the buyer away (b) lower your asking price to $90,000 or (c) owner finance the additional $10,000 for your buyer, meaning you would hold a second or junior lien on the property.

In this example, the house sells for $100,000 - the buyer puts down a $10,000 deposit leaving a balance of $90,000. They borrow $80,000 from a mortgage lender who then holds the first lien against the property. They borrow the final $10,000 from you and you have a second or junior lien against the property. As in the first example, they would repay your $10,000 exactly as the terms state in the promissory note you and your attorney create, have signed, and record.

Advantages of owner financing

There are many benefits to both the buyer and the seller for owner financing as opposed to conventional lending. Consider: Do you really need the cash from the sale in a lump sum today? Would it work for you to spread the income from your property out over time, with interest?

Benefits for the seller

- **Getting a better price**—You, the seller, should receive full market value when offering flexible owner-financed terms. Buyers will pay a premium for not having to qualify for traditional financing.

- **Getting the house sold**—If you make a portion of the loan on the property, the borrower needs less from a mortgage company meaning that a larger number of people will be able to qualify for the amount needed to purchase your property. If you finance the entire selling price, buyers don't need to qualify for a loan at all. This greatly increases the number of people interested in your property and a larger buyer pool means a faster sale.

- **Faster closing**—Offers are usually contingent upon the buyer obtaining financing, meaning that, after you have a signed contract, your buyer still may not qualify for enough to purchase the property. An owner-financed transaction, however, can close in a matter of days since there is no loan approval, appraisal, underwriting, or survey involved.

- **Savings**—You can save thousands in closing costs, title insurance, and the balance of your existing financing.

- **Tax advantages**—You should realize tax advantages because your payments come in over time rather than getting your profit all in one lump sum. You only pay tax on the gains you receive each year as you receive them.

- **Creating income**—Owner financing creates ongoing monthly income for you and, possibly, your heirs.

- **Interest income**—Like any other lender, you can charge interest on the money you lend to the buyer. Collecting this interest over time increases the total amount you gain from the sale.

> *Like any other lender, you can charge interest on the money you are lending to the buyer. Collecting this interest over time increases the total amount you gain from the sale.*

- **Protection**—To protect yourself, you can require the buyer to make monthly payments into an escrow account held by a bank, attorney, or other lending institution.

- **Secure Asset**—You can require the borrower to place a quitclaim deed into the escrow account stating that, if a payment is late by a certain number of days, the escrow officer automatically files the quitclaim deed, returning the house back to you.

If this happens, the buyer not only loses the property, but all payments they made on the property as well. This is a powerful incentive for the buyer to perform as agreed.

Benefits for the buyer

- **Easier qualification**—If the seller is willing to make a portion of the loan on the property, buyers have a much easier time qualifying for a loan.

- **No income or credit screening**—Owner financing does not require traditional income or credit approval. Many things can hurt a buyer's credit; divorce, illness, self-employment. All of these obstacles can disappear with owner financing.

- **Fewer costs**—When receiving seller financing, points, origination fees, and closing costs may be negotiated or eliminated, saving them potentially thousands of dollars.

> *When receiving seller financing, the buyer has no points, origination fees, appraiser fees or other closing costs to pay, saving them potentially thousands of dollars.*

- **Lower interest rate**—While you may charge the same interest rate that a bank or other financial institution would charge, a buyer may negotiate a lower interest rate through you.

- **Fewer restrictions**—Many more aspects of the purchase are open to negotiation than when dealing with a traditional lender such as credit history, down payment and debt to income ratio.

- **Time**—Owner financing gives the buyer time to improve their credit score while creating a history of on-time payments. When your balloon becomes due in say three to five years, the buyer is then able to qualify for traditional financing because of his or her improved credit.

- **Faster closing**—The buyer is able to move in a matter of days rather than the months of wait involved with traditional financing.

Wrap-around loan

Do you have an outstanding loan balance on your property? Perhaps you can do what's called a wrap-around loan or wrap-around mortgage.

With a wrap-around, you as the seller lend the buyer the difference between your existing loan and the purchase price. The buyer's monthly loan payments are sufficient to repay your existing loan as well as your new loan to the buyer.

Can you see all the advantages to both you and the buyer with owner financing? Is this something you can offer?

Chapter 7

SELLING WITH A LEASE OPTION

S ometimes, after doing all the calculations, people find their home is worth less on today's retail market than the amount still owed to the lender.

If this is true for you and you're not quite able to sell but leery of renting, is there some middle ground? Actually, there is. Lease-to-own is a great bridge until you can sell.

How is lease-to-own different from a rental?

Lease-to-own works very much like a rental but with some of the benefits of buying. The buyer does not, however, have to qualify up front through a traditional lender.

Similar to renting, the tenant/buyer (lessee) moves into a property owned by someone else and pays a monthly amount to live there. The difference with a lease-to-own is that the lessee is actually working toward owning that home at a future date.

The contracts signed include terms for both the rental agreement and the lease agreement. The additional lease terms spell out conditions for the future purchase of the home such as:

1. The amount of time the lessee has to purchase (typically 12–36 months)

2. The purchase price of the home (which is locked in for the term of the contract)

3. The amount of the lease option fee (or "down payment" to move in)

4. Any possible seller financing terms

5. The amount of monthly credit toward purchase given for on-time payments (if any)

6. Any other terms or conditions of the lease

The lease option fee actually "buys" the lessee the right to purchase the home at a future date and locks in the purchase price. It is typically required at time of contract signing, and a portion of or the entire lease option fee may be credited toward the purchase price. If the contract is not fulfilled, the lease option fee is forfeited and the "buyer" moves on.

The great thing about a lease for the lessees is that they know they have a contract toward buying the home they live in. While the lease option is in effect, the home cannot be sold to someone else (which is one of the risks with a rental). This gives lessees time to save a down payment and improve their credit scores before getting a loan.

Qualifying to buy another property

Is it possible you can rent out the house you have now and purchase another home? As a matter of fact, if you can prove to a lender that you have a tenant in the property and you're not responsible for the monthly payment, after six to twelve months you can qualify to buy another property.

That is, of course, if everything else on your credit report is satisfactory. If you qualify for a loan now, chances are you will still qualify when you convert your current home to a rental rather than selling it. The lender will credit 75 percent to 80 percent of the rental income you receive from your tenant to offset the expense of your property. If you're able to rent it out for more than your monthly overhead, that income can actually wash out the expense of your rental property on your new loan application.

This allows you to hold the property until the market turns around, and then sell for a profit at a future date. Remember, you don't lose money on it until you sell.

Not interested in being a landlord? Hire a property management company. But before you do, check them out to make sure they're reputable and compare their services with others in your area.

If your house is not selling, don't think you have to walk away, allow it to go to foreclosure, or attempt a short sale. All of these "solutions" will cost time and money and will negatively affect your credit. Putting in a tenant who can cover the monthly overhead on your current home is an excellent way to avoid taking a loss in the current real estate market.

> *Putting in a tenant who can cover the monthly overhead on your current home is an excellent way to avoid taking a loss in the current real estate market.*

Lease option is a great bridge between renting and owning

The lessee experiences a pride of ownership that a renter does not, while still having the flexibility of a rental. If at any time the lessee decides not to purchase the property, he or she can forfeit their deposit, move on and the contract ends.

If you find you can't sell your home, don't give up. Leasing your home to the future buyer may be your perfect alternative.

Chapter 8

12 OPTIONS FOR SELLERS FACING FORECLOSURE

U nderstanding your options is important when negotiating. Just because you've gotten a foreclosure notice, don't panic and move your belongings to the curb. Be informed, get active, and make the best decision for you and your family.

Most of the following options are available to qualifying sellers. The exact terms may vary from these definitions, but this is a guideline of possibilities to discuss with your lender. As a general rule, your lender wants payment, not the property, so the possibility always exists that you can work something out.

With all work-outs, you will be required to prove hardships and justifiable reasons for your request.

> *Your lender wants payment, not the property, so the possibility always exists that you can work something out.*

12 Options when Facing Foreclosure

1. **Reinstatement:** Paying the loan balance off in a very short time, usually within 24 months. Total reinstatement involves paying the lender everything that is owed in one lump sum including missed payments and all fees.

   For most of us, I know this first one sounds far fetched. If they can pay off the loan balance, why are they in trouble? But, there are times when monies can be found through a family member, business partner, etc., allowing the borrower to fully pay off the loan. Perhaps even an investor would be willing to step in and purchase your property by paying off your loan balance. These types of transactions do happen.

2. **Repayment plan:** These plans typically require higher payments than your regular monthly mortgage amount for a period of time until the loan is brought up to date.

   For example, your monthly payment is $1,000 and your past due amount is $5,600. The lender agrees to take monthly payments from you of $1,200 until the past due (plus any fees they may add) is paid in full. Once the past due or "arrearages" are paid, your monthly payment drops again to $1,000.

3. **Loan modification:** Involves changing one or more terms of a mortgage. Possible modifications include:

   - Reducing the interest rate of the mortgage

   - Changing the mortgage terms (i.e., from an adjustable rate to a fixed rate)

   - Lowering monthly payments by extending the term of the mortgage

   - Adding past-due payments plus fees to the back end of the loan

When helping homeowners with modifications, we have been fairly successful getting lenders to move past due amounts plus fees to the back end of the loan. What this offers lenders is a longer payment term and the opportunity to collect more interest. For the borrower, the past-due amounts are no longer an immediate cause for concern.

> *When helping homeowners with modifications, we have been fairly successful getting lenders to move past due amounts plus fees to the back end of the loan.*

4. **Forbearance:** The lender allows a short time period of either low payments or no payments at all. This means later payments will be higher than the original monthly payments until the loan is, once again, up to date.

5. **Special forbearance (FHA Loans only):** Allows FHA borrowers to postpone monthly mortgage payments for at least four months. There is no maximum number of months allowed, however, the delinquency may never exceed the equivalent of twelve monthly PITI (principle, interest, taxes, insurance) payments. So, while there is no maximum number of months, there is a maximum delinquent dollar amount allowed.

6. **Deed-in-lieu:** The borrower voluntarily deeds the property back to the lender in exchange for a release from all obligations of the mortgage.

    Deed-in-lieu may sound like a fabulous idea, but you must check with the lender to see if they're willing to receive the property back. A deed-in-lieu must be agreed to by both the borrower and the lender.

A deed-in-lieu immediately releases the borrower from the mortgage debt and has less impact on credit than a foreclosure. For the lender, it is less costly and time consuming than a foreclosure.

> *A deed-in-lieu immediately releases the borrower from the mortgage debt and has less impact on credit than a foreclosure.*

7. **Cash sale:** The borrower sells the property, pays off the loan, and may even receive some profit. This is a retail transaction and requires you to sell quickly enough and at a price high enough to pay off the loan.

   If you're facing foreclosure and hope to sell your home on the retail market to avoid it, don't delay—market your property immediately!

8. **Short sale:** The borrower makes an agreement with the lender to sell for less than the full amount owed. This generally results in no cash to you, the homeowner, but is better for your credit than a foreclosure. Short sales are discussed in Chapter 4, Short Sale.

9. **Refinance:** Getting a new loan. This requires that you have both good credit and equity in the property.

10. **Selling "subject-to" your existing financing**: With a subject-to transaction, you deed the property to an investor/buyer "subject-to" your existing loan, allowing the investor/buyer to pay it off at a later date. Your buyer is then on the recorded deed as owner of the property, yet you remain on the loan and maintain the ultimate responsibility for the loan repayment.

    One risk is, once a buyer takes your property subject-to, the lender may call the loan due immediately because of the due on sale clause in your mortgage documents. You, the seller, no longer own the property (it was deeded to the buyer when they took over the property) and you have no recourse if the buyer doesn't make the payments. Because your name remains on the loan, non-payment hurts your credit, not the buyer's.

As a general rule, lenders do not call these loans due. Why? Because they want the regular payments to continue; they do not want the property.

We make these purchases on a regular basis. It is a legitimate, legal way to purchase properties. No matter how you sell your property, at closing both you and the buyer receive a HUD-1 Settlement Statement itemizing all fees associated with transferring the property. The HUD-1 is a government form (U.S. Department of Housing and Urban Development) and you will find subject-to amounts itemized on lines 203 in the borrower's column and 503 in the seller's column. HUD-1 will be discussed in Chapter 22, Closing Costs.

You will find subject-to amounts itemized on lines 203 and 503 of the HUD-1 Settlement Statement.

When considering selling subject-to, it is imperative that you research to know the buyer. We, for example, have offices, lots of customer testimonials, are listed with the Better Business Bureau, and our business practices can be traced back for years. A seller can research our company and be comfortable that we are credible, will continue to make the payments to the lender as promised, and are not going away.

We also state in our contracts that, should anything prevent us from making the scheduled mortgage payments, property ownership will revert back to the mortgage holder. The advantage to mortgage holders is that they would get the property back with any updates we've added plus the advantage of the mortgage pay-down from the time we took the property over. We have never returned a property and certainly never intend to do so, but the assurance gives comfort to the seller.

Should you decide to sell subject-to, make sure you have checked out the buyer and have similar protections in place. Subject-to may be the perfect scenario to allow you to sell quickly.

11. **Do nothing:** The worst choice as your credit will be ruined. This does, however, allow you to stay in the house for months without paying. You can save cash and not move until the lender or new purchaser finally evicts.

12. **Rent:** How about putting a tenant in your property and moving to something more affordable? Can you rent the property out for enough to cover your current property expenses, or at least enough to allow you to move on with your life and prevent foreclosure?

We discussed option 12 in Chapter 3, Rent Your Home or Sell It. Renting may be a solution that allows you to move on with the peace of mind that your property and credit scores are intact.

Section Three

PREPARING TO SELL

I s there anything you can do to help get your house sold? Absolutely! And, the more you do, the faster you'll sell and the higher the sales price can be.

In this section, I cover a number of helpful preparations including renovations, landscaping, and getting your documents in order. If doing one of these ideas would be good, doing ALL of them would be GREAT!

You're already ahead of your selling competition just by picking up this book. Most sellers don't know what to do or how to do it. They rely on their agent and many agents aren't that experienced and don't have the knowledge you'll gain here.

So, read these principles, apply them, and get your house SOLD!

> *If doing one of these ideas would be good, doing ALL of them would be GREAT!*

Section Three

Chapter 9

PREPARING YOUR HOME TO SELL

eads up: Just because you decide to put your house on the market does not mean it will sell right away.

Just because you love your home and the way it's decorated does not mean the prospect who walks through the door will feel the same way.

Selling your home can be emotional and you have to know that going in so you can be prepared in case the process becomes more difficult than you expect.

You can't control some things such as location or market conditions; however, you can control your asking price, the condition of your property, and how much marketing you're willing to do. Here are some tips on how to do just that.

Get a fresh perspective

It's hard to look at your home objectively so:

1. **Have a friend or neighbor give suggestions**. What things would they want changed or what makes them uncomfortable? Something simple that you may not think about,

like the room being crowded or worn carpeting, other people will notice.

You can't control some things such as location or market conditions; however, you can control your asking price, the condition of your property, and how much marketing you're willing to do.

2. **Be open to what your agent has to say**. Real estate agents market properties for a living and know what buyers look for, what they notice, and what your competitors are doing to sell their properties.

3. **Take photos of your home**, interior and exterior. It may be easier to see what needs to be done when looking at a picture.

4. **Enlist the aid of a buyer.** Invite someone who has not seen your home before to come through and give their first impression. Do you have a co-worker who is looking for a home? Ask them to look at yours through their "buyer eyes."

14 Quick Preparation Tips:

1. **Curb appeal**—You don't want a potential buyer's first vision of your home to be negative. ("Look how much work it's going to be to keep up this yard.") So, no matter what the season, have the yard mowed, trimmed and neat, and remove anything dead.

2. **Front door**—At the very least, make sure it's clean. You may want to replace or paint the front door as this is your potential buyer's first up-close look at the property. Make sure storm doors are clean and that all locks and door handles are tight and functioning. A loose or broken lock gives a bad impression before prospects even enter your home.

3. **Light**—Make sure you home looks spacious and light. If you have darker areas in the house, buy additional lamps for those spaces. Put in full wattage bulbs (check the tag on the lamp neck for maximum allowable wattage) and make sure all bulbs in the house work. When the house is being shown, have ALL lights on, even closet lights and the one over the stove. Light and bright makes your home much more desirable.

4. **Windows**—Open drapes and blinds to let in as much natural light as possible. Take down all worn, torn, or broken blinds or drapes. Anything worn, torn, or broken will knock a lot off the buyer's offer and you can be sure they're deducting as they walk through. Bare windows look far better than windows with torn or dirty treatments. And make sure windows are clean. Clean windows let in more light, improve the view on the other side, and make the rest of the house feel cleaner.

5. **Clean**—The home must be clean. If you don't plan to paint the entire interior and replace all the carpets, make sure what is there is clean. Put everything in its place.

6. **De-personalize**—You want buyers to see themselves and their family living in the house. It's important to take down family photos, trophies, collectibles, anything that makes them see this as your home, not theirs.

7. **Smell/fragrance/odor?**—This will be the first thing prospects notice when they walk in. You certainly don't want the house to smell musty or like last night's dinner. Scrub well and consider lemon scented cleaning products or vanilla scented candles.

8. **Pets**—Remove pets and traces of pets including beds, toys, and odor. Many buyers do not like pets and will leave a home without consideration if they see that a pet lives there.

9. **Clutter**—No. None. Clean out, throw away, and store everything you can. Now's the time to get rid of things you don't

want, but don't replace them! Much better to have your home look open and spacious.

10. **Furniture**—Don't let your home feel crowded. This gives the buyer the impression that there's not enough space for their things. If you have a lot and can't get rid of the excess, rent a storage building and take out more than you think you should. You may find you actually enjoy the extra space.

11. **Bathrooms**—Remove everything you use—toothbrush, toothpaste, hairbrushes, combs, razors, shampoo, bar soaps, makeup, everything—out of the shower and off the vanities. The bathroom should be so clean it sparkles. Hang a new shower curtain—clear or white—and leave it open so the bathroom looks larger. Make sure all light bulbs are working and the highest wattage possible. No one likes a dingy or dirty bathroom. It's best to install new toilet seats (very inexpensive) and, if necessary, new faucets and showerheads. Clean all grout. Great grout cleaners can be found at home improvement stores.

12. **Kitchen**—Remove everything from countertops to make the space look as large as possible. Scrub all appliances until they shine. No water spots or stains in the sink. Take everything off the refrigerator—notes, photos, magnets, everything. Make sure cabinets and doors are free from fingerprints. Dated hardware? You can really spruce up your cabinets by replacing the knobs. Check out Habitat for Humanity stores for great deals on cabinet hardware.

13. **Bedrooms**—Neat, clean, beds made, and no clutter. Removing an extra nightstand or dresser may do wonders for increasing the visual space of the room.

Make closets look as large as possible by leaving at least 30 percent of the space vacant.

14. **Closets**—In every room of the house, clean out closets by throwing out or passing on anything not still being used. Make closets look as large as possible by leaving at least 30 percent of the space vacant. If necessary, pack up and store what you don't need now, anything out of season. When buyers open doors, you want them to see plenty of closet space in the home.

> *Make sure your home is available to show anytime a buyer is ready to view it.*

Finally, make sure your home is available to show anytime there is a buyer ready to view it. This puts you ahead of the other sellers who only want to show when it's convenient for them. If it's difficult to schedule a showing appointment, buyers and agents will move onto the next home and the chances with that prospect are lost. Be accommodating. Make sure your home is readily available.

Chapter 10

REHABBING TIPS AND TRICKS

ere's a question I get often: *"Other than price, what rehab makes the most difference?"*

Here are some things we've found that help sell quickly.

1. **Landscaping**—Start here so people driving by are immediately interested, even while you're renovating. Cleaning up the yard and front of the house first also thrills the neighbors and gets them talking positively. "Face lift" landscaping is fast and easy—pull out weeds, throw down pine needles. A bit of aeration and seed can mean new grass by the time the house is ready for the for-sale sign.

2. **Front door and the entry hardware**—This is the first up-close viewing of your property. Make sure both the door and door knob are in excellent condition – that the knob is tight and works well and that the door not only looks good but opens and closes efficiently. Something as subtle as a loose

doorknob or squeaky hinges puts the buyer on alert from the time they enter, even if only subconsciously.

3. **Crown molding**—This subtle fix adds a great deal of impact. If your budget allows, add it to main living areas such as living and dining rooms.

4. **Replace fixtures**—Light fixtures are inexpensive and new ones work wonders, as do new door and drawer knobs. Old knobs that have paint slopped on them need cleaning or replacing. Plumbing fixtures are more expensive than lighting but make a significant visual difference.

5. **Mirrors**—A quick, inexpensive change that is always noticed is to take out standard sheet mirrors in bathrooms and replace them with nice framed mirrors.

6. **Paint**—When painting, give the trim a contrasting color from the walls. If you don't want much of a contrast, make walls at least two shades darker or lighter than the trim for an extra pop. Gloss paint for the trim makes them easy to wipe off. Don't paint walls gloss, however, or every bump and crack will show when the lights are on.

   I read a quote: *"A gallon of paint may cost $20, but, when applied correctly, it can be worth $200 in the price of the home."* I don't want to guarantee a $200 return, but you get the point. Pay special attention to the "when applied correctly" part. Buyers will scrutinize your property and a bad paint job with wall paint on the ceiling, the trim, or the flooring, can actually take away from the value you're trying to add.

7. **Painting Interior Brick**—I love this. In almost every house we renovate, I paint brick fireplaces and hearths. Most brick is old and unattractive. Besides, who ever cleans brick? Paint fireplaces the same color as the wall. They seem to disappear and the room is immediately larger. I paint the interiors black (make sure it's paint that will handle the heat of the fires) and the whole unit looks clean and beautiful.

Paint the mantels the same color as the rest of the trim in the room.

8. **Replace electrical outlet covers**—Once you've painted, be sure to replace outlet covers. Dingy, old switch and outlet covers really stand out on clean walls and make prospects wonder what else you've glossed over.

9. **Caulk**—Inexpensive and easy to use. When done correctly, caulk makes areas look tight, neat and clean. Especially important around tubs, showers and sinks to prevent leaks.

10. **Nasty tile colors**—If tiles are in good shape, they can be painted any color you like. We have ours done professionally, tubs as well, as the kits you buy at home improvement centers tend to chip and peel over time. The ones we have done professionally look like new and never go bad.

11. **Continuity**—Whether your prefer brass, brushed nickel, shiny, matt, or antique, best to have all knobs, light fixtures, plumbing fixtures, and hinges match. Many of the things I'm listing make a subliminal impact and the buyer may not even know what it is they like or don't like, but your attention to detail will pay big dividends.

    Your attention to detail will pay big dividends.

12. **Changing kitchen cabinets**—In our experience, new sells much faster than painting old ones. New cabinets look new and painted cabinets look like a quick and less expensive fix. Painting the outside doesn't make the inside look better and buyers know what was done. They, again, wonder what else you simply covered up.

13. **Kitchens and baths**—The most important feature of any house so make sure yours sparkle. Even if you're not replacing anything, these are the two areas of the house that must be absolutely clean.

14. **Inexpensive blinds**—At the very least, put up inexpensive blinds so exterior openings can be covered and your prospects don't see the added expense of window treatments. With blinds, your buyer can move in and sleep in the home immediately.

15. **Light bulbs**—I almost omitted this because it seems so obvious, but you must have working light bulbs in all fixtures including appliances and the one over the stove. Really.

16. **Garage floor**—One of my favorites and the one that always gets oohs and ahhhs, is a clean and painted garage floor. Yup, cleaning out and painting the garage makes the whole house seem new. Don't miss the floor. Concrete paint is cheap.

17. **Siding**—Buyers prefer siding to exterior paint because it's less expensive to maintain.

18. **Decks and porches**—Pressure wash and stain decks so the whole house looks and feels fresh.

19. **Crawl space**—Remember to check under the house. Yes, this too, needs to be clean and neat. Laying down plastic adds a more attended to look and protects the house from moisture.

20. **Mailbox**—Last, but not least, a new mailbox and painted or replaced post. Everyone sees it; you want it to look new.

Best and worst rehab choices for the money

Does your home need more than a little sprucing up? Are the colors, carpets, appliances, and window treatments dated? We're constantly asked, *"What should I do to this property to get the most return for my investment?"*

Great question! And, before you begin any rehab on a property you plan to sell, investigate the return you can expect versus the amount you'll spend.

For example, if you plan to spend $40,000 adding a sunroom, would you still do it if it would only raise your property value $15,000? Following are some of the best and worst ideas we've used.

1. **Upkeep**—Probably the best advice for the least money is to keep up the property while you live in it. Many sellers go all out fixing broken cabinet doors, cracked windows, exterior paint, replacing blinds, etc., when they plan to move. Really? Why let your house deteriorate in the first place? Keeping your home in top condition allows you to love it while you're there, keeps upkeep costs low and spread out, and when you decide to sell, it's practically ready "as is."

2. **Landscaping**—Big bang for your buck here. Clean up the yard and clear out anything dead or dying. Aerate the soil, spread grass seed and put mulch or straw around shrubs. If the season is right, buy some inexpensive plants for color.

3. **Home office**—There was a time when home office was a big selling point. Now, with laptops and iPads, the office can be anywhere there's a comfortable place to sit. Homeowners prefer an extra bedroom to a room with built in bookcases and high-tech wiring that limits its use. If you have a home office space, do what you can to make that room more versatile for buyers.

   Surveys tell you to expect only a 50 percent return on money you invest in a large master bath upgrade.

4. **Master suites**—Yes, buyers love them. Buyers, in fact, look for master bedrooms with attached master baths that include jetted tubs, tile floors, double vanities, and enclosed showers. However, if your home doesn't currently have one, you probably don't have the space to add it. And, guess what? Companies that

survey this type of thing tell you to expect only a 50 percent return on money you invest in a large master bath upgrade. Yes, buyers want them and will buy a newer home that has one, but they aren't going to pay you back for your remodel.

5. **Additional bathroom**—Buyers want at minimum two full baths and prefer an additional half bath for guests. Don't have one? By adding square footage for another bath, again expect only a 50 percent return on your investment. A better and less expensive option is if you have a closet or space that allows you to add one in your existing square footage. Bathrooms are very high on buyers' lists of wants, but keep your costs down because they also want a deal of a purchase price.

6. **Garage**—Most people prefer a garage, especially in colder climates. But adding an attached, two-car garage can cost $70,000. Will that overprice your home for the neighborhood? Buyers want to know they got a bargain, so you can't ask more than your neighborhood comparables allow. Expect about a 50 percent return on money spent to add a garage.

7. **Already have a garage?**—A fabulous selling tip is to clean it out, totally, so buyers see all that additional storage space. Rent a storage room if necessary in order to empty your garage. When cleaned out, put up drywall if your garage has only studs, and paint the walls so it looks fresh and clean. For the total new garage renovation, go to your home improvement store and get what you need to clean the floor of all grease. Paint the cleaned floor with grey concrete paint and that like-new space will do wonders toward selling your home quickly.

8. **Paint**—Again, very inexpensive for the results it produces. See where it's needed inside your home as well as out. But, paint well - a sloppy paint job will not add value.

In Summary

When rehabbing, always keep in mind how you would feel as the buyer. You will expect the home to look great, be in good shape, and have systems (i.e., heat and air, hot water) that function. These are items you *expect*, not extras you pay for.

So, remember, even though you spent thousands on landscaping, buyers may hate it and be calculating the cost to replace it.

Even though you spent extra on stainless steel appliances, buyers may prefer black.

And, even though you just put in a new furnace and want to recoup the expense, buyers expect the house to have heat!

> *To sell your house as quickly as possible, have it in the condition you would want if you were buying.*

To sell your house as quickly as possible, have it in the condition you would want if you were buying. The buyer may not want to pay for all your updates, but they're still necessary to get your house sold.

Chapter 11

LANDSCAPING ADDS VALUE

You've probably heard of the importance of curb appeal.
Yes, it's VERY important. You want prospective buyers
to at least enter the house! Many buyers decide NOT
to buy simply based on the exterior appearance. If the exterior looks bad, understandably they assume that the house
itself was not well maintained.

However . . .

How much value can landscaping add?

You can actually increase the value of your home by improving the landscaping. An old *Money Magazine* survey found that
good landscaping can add 7 percent to 14 percent to the value of
your home.

An American Society of Landscape Architects study found
that homeowners may receive 100 percent or more of the money
they invest in professional landscaping services when they sell.
The U.S. Forest Service says that trees alone add at least 3 percent
to property values.

No matter the source of these numbers, you get the point.
Landscaping offers a huge return-on-investment, one of the

highest I've found! It seems that money spent on well-done landscaping is worth it for:

Landscaping is one of the highest return-on-investment remodeling tips I've found!

1. The value of your home

2. Curb appeal, which helps with selling

3. The aesthetic enjoyment for yourself, your family, and your neighbors

4. The health of the environment

Look around for landscaping you like, even in local parks, find out who did the work, and contact them for pricing. Get referrals, check their previous work, and plan to do something special for your home! As a bonus, until it's sold you've created a beautiful yard as your private retreat and a comfortable spot to come home to.

Ten tips for a better yard

When selling, first impressions are everything. Make someone fall in love with your home the minute they pull up to the front.

Here are ten easy landscape suggestions:

1. **Problem areas**—If you have problem areas in your yard, test the pH levels. You can send a soil sample to your county or state's extension service—just Google for your state resource. This process can take six weeks, so if you don't want to wait, check around. I found a local garden nursery that will test my soil for free and I had my results in less than ten minutes!

2. **Trim shrubs**—Keep plants at least a foot away from the house to allow air circulation which prevents mold and rot. Always remove anything dead or dying.

3. **Spread mulch**—Around trees, shrubs, and planted areas. Mulch, bark, or pine needles help keep weeds down and gives the yard a clean "finished" look. Mulches fade and settle over time from the sun and rain, so reapply each spring.

4. **Edge flowerbeds**—Makes your yard look neat and groomed.

5. **Power wash**—Or at least go around with a broom to get down cobwebs, mold, and dirt from everything—decks, patios, fences, trellises, windows, siding, and brick. Having your home pressure washed is fairly inexpensive or you can rent a pressure washer and do it yourself. Caution - don't get water under the siding, in soffits, or in vents where it can cause damage.

   * Heads-up: After you have pressure washed your home, the exterior of your windows will need cleaning!

6. **Plant flowers**—I prefer perennials because they come up year after year and I don't have the expense or effort of repurchasing and replanting every spring. I plant a few annuals (they won't come back) like coleus to add all-season color as most flowering plants bloom for only a short time. Coleus thrives well, is low maintenance, and adds gorgeous color and impact. Hanging baskets are great, not only in entry areas and on porches but also hanging on hooks in the yard or from tree branches.

7. **Plant a garden**—If you have a sunny spot, a small bed with veggies adds so much! It's beautiful, it's great exercise, and you end up with wonderful, wholesome edibles! I prefer edible plants anywhere they will grow. I plant fruit trees that flower in the spring and I can pick from in the summer and fall. I have herbs growing everywhere: fragrant lavender

under our windows; creeping thyme and rosemary along and through the stone staircase; sage, parsley, chamomile, and basil filling in bare spaces in shrub areas.

* Caution: Plant mint in containers as mint loves to wander!

8. **Hang a hammock**—Nothing suggests easy living like a hammock. If you don't have two trees close enough to string one between, use a hammock stand. Ours is always a big hit with guests.

9. **Create conversation areas**—Not just on your deck but also in your yard. I have a metal bench in a front area, a stone bench in another area and tables and chairs on the deck. These provide lots of comfortable space to enjoy Mother Nature. Make your yard another usable area of your home.

> *Make your yard another usable area of your home.*

10. **Mowing**—When caring for your lawn, set your mower high (at least three inches). Higher grass reduces stress, cuts down on the need for water, and helps choke out weeds. The higher the grass, the deeper the roots and the more resilient grass is in hot sun.

Selling or staying, landscaping adds value to your home. You can't lose with good landscaping. Invest, enjoy, and reap the rewards!

Chapter 12

COSTS TO SELL YOUR HOME

S ome sellers actually believe they will be "getting" what they sell their house for and are shocked at closing by the number on their side of the HUD-1 Settlement Statement (ask any closing attorney). Warning! There are tremendous costs to sell.

What costs will you incur when you sell?

1. To begin with, don't expect to get your asking price. In this economy, a 5 percent discount is conservative. So, if you list your home for $200,000 don't let an offer of $180,000 be a surprise.

2. Don't forget to deduct real estate commission from your proceeds. I'm always amazed when sellers, who know about this cost, don't deduct it mentally from what they will receive at closing. Real estate commission is a true expense if you have your house listed with a real estate agent or if an agent brings you a buyer. The commission you've agreed to pay will be deducted from your side of the settlement statement.

3. Inspections—Every home inspector will find needed repairs (that's what they're paid to do) and most sellers have no idea how much those repairs are going to cost. Especially in today's real estate market, buyers want all those items repaired.

4. Pest inspections—Insects such as termites, not neighbors.

5. Home shield—A service contract that covers the repair or replacement of some of the most frequently occurring break-downs of certain home system components, i.e., heating and air conditioner units and appliances. The service contract is good for one year and today's buyers expect this to be provided by the seller.

6. Then there are recording fees, attorney fees, sometimes a survey, transfer tax (varies by state, even county), document prep fees, title insurance, courier fees, etc. These fees typically total 3 percent to 5 percent of the selling price of your home.

A quick formula we use for determining costs to sell is:

- Start with your asking price.

- Be realistic and expect your offer to be 7 percent lower— subtract 7 percent.

- Take that selling price and subtract 6 percent for the agent commission.

- Deduct another 3 percent for closing costs.

- Finally, subtract 4 percent for the necessary repairs.

And, don't forget to calculate the cost of moving to a new home.

Can you afford to sell for the price you come up with using this formula? If not, can you put off selling your home for now? If you need to move now, is renting your house out something you can

Don't forget to calculate the cost of moving to a new home.

consider? We discussed this in Chapter 8, Selling Your Home with a Lease Option.

Which option works for you?

Chapter 13

GETTING YOUR DOCUMENTATION IN ORDER

A s you prepare to market your property, there is information you should have readily available for prospective buyers as well as for your agent and, ultimately, the closing. These items may be needed to justify your asking price, as well as being important documents to pass onto your buyer.

Armed with this information, an agent, title company, or closing attorney will be better able to assist you with your transaction.

The more information you provide from the beginning of the process, the more time and effort you will ultimately save.

What documentation do you need?

1. **Survey**—Of your property to confirm boundary and easement locations.

2. **Mortgage information**—Current loan(s), information including name(s) and address(es) of lender(s) as well as account number(s), payment amount(s), and due date(s).

3. **Dates**—When you replaced or had serviced items such as roof, water heater, heating and air system, appliances, etc.

4. **A binder or manual of warranties**—For your appliances, HVAC, water heater, roof, etc.

5. **Vendor contact information**—For annual services performed such as servicing the HVAC, pest treatment, or lawn care.

6. **Utilities**—Names and addresses of companies (gas, electric, water, cable, etc.) and average rates for last twelve months.

7. **Well and Septic**—Information if applicable.

8. **Security System**—Verify company information and term of service.

9. **Neighborhood information**—Location of shopping, schools, police, and fire, as well as contact information for people in the neighborhood.

10. **HOA information**—A copy of the covenants, monthly fees, address for payments, contact person and this person's contact information.

11. **History of your property**—Any pertinent information regarding the history of your property, such as the builder, house plans, and information regarding additions prior to your purchasing the home, etc.

12. **Upgrades**—Which amenities you have added to your home.

13. **Your proposed sales price**—And how you determined it.

14. **Return On Investment (ROI)**—How much are you expecting for these upgrades? How much did you spend for these items and how much of the expense do you hope to get back? How did you come up with that number? You may have added improvements to your home, for example a pool, hot tub, or room addition, that will not actually add value to the property or certainly not dollar for dollar what you spent.

15. **If property has rental units involved**—Make sure to have copies of all leases, rents, and deposits that will transfer with sale.

16. **Keys**—Have working keys for all locks including garage doors, sliding doors and storage buildings. Have extra keys made to use in the property lock box.

Some of these items, such as the property survey, may be found in the closing packet you received when you purchased your home.

Your goal is a swift and easy transaction. The more information you provide from the beginning of the process, the more time and effort you will ultimately save.

Section Four

MARKETING

First and foremost in getting any property sold—anywhere, in any condition—is marketing.

If buyers don't know what you have, where it is, how much it costs, or even that it's for sale, what are your odds of selling it? Thus the need to market, market, market.

In this section, I'll go from determining your true property value all the way to having an open house.

> *If buyers don't know what you have, where it is, how much it costs, or even that it's for sale, what are your odds of selling it?*

Chapter 14

DETERMINING YOUR PROPERTY VALUE

What is your home really worth and who makes that final decision?

You think it should be worth more than you paid for it. Your listing agent offers to list it for higher than you need so, hopefully, your buyer will pay enough for you to walk away with profit. The buyer wants to buy at what the messed up foreclosure down the street is selling for. The lender wants an "accurate" appraisal from a licensed appraiser.

Problem is, home sellers and appraisers argue over true valuations. Who's right? Who wins? How do you know?

Actually, you can list your home for any price you like. Some sellers use what they paid for the house, add what they've spent on improvements, and then add an amount for profit. Some list based on what they need to pay off their mortgage balance, closing costs, plus the real estate agent commission.

To move a property quickly, you may be tempted to list below others in your neighborhood. If you add the REOs (foreclosed properties) to the mix, housing prices can be all over the place even in the same neighborhood.

Let's discuss better and more accurate options for pricing your home.

Actually, you can list your home for any price you like.

Online sites to help determine home values

There are many free sites (free is good) and some are, of course, better than others. Try different ones until you find the ones you prefer.

- **Zillow.com** is a popular site and quick resource for property information. This is good for comping an entire area because, once you put in an address, surrounding homes pop up with price estimates on every roof.

- **RealEstateABC.com** gives a fantastic chart of recent area sales.

- **Realestate.com** works to look up properties listed by real estate agents.

- **Trulia.com** is another popular site for property information, stats, and trends.

There are two main methods for determining property values: comparable sales and cost per square foot.

Determining property value

You're ready to sell and you know what you owe. But how do you know what it's worth? Agents as well as potential buyers will also be working to justify your asking price. There are two main methods for determining property values: comparable sales and cost per square foot.

Comparable sales (comps)

Comparable sales are the most commonly used method to determine property value. By comparing similar characteristics between homes of comparable size, value, age, and location, you are better able to determine the true value of your property.

Four key factors when comping properties

Many factors come into play when comping properties, but four key factors are location, size (square footage), number of bedrooms and bathrooms, and condition. Many more details are considered by professional appraisers to get a "true" value, but these four factors are easy to use, easy to find, and will give you a good idea of the value of your property.

1. **Location.** You may have heard that, in real estate, the main three things to consider for value are location, location, and location! Location is extremely important when comparing properties. Where possible, consider only homes in your same neighborhood or within a one-quarter to one-half mile radius.

2. **Size.** Appraisers prefer to use homes with no more than 20 percent more or less in square footage than the target property. If your property has 1,000 square feet, look at similar homes that are 800–1,200 square feet. The closer in size, of course, the better. If there is nothing of similar size nearby, use the cost per square foot method, which I'll cover shortly.

3. **Bedrooms and bathrooms.** The number of bedrooms and bathrooms is extremely important. A three-bedroom home with 1,200 square feet might be worth more than a two-bedroom home with 1,300 square feet. It also matters where the bedrooms and bathrooms are located. For example, the

main floor is preferred; the basement is not so good. At least one bedroom on the main level is highly desirable.

Three-bedroom homes are generally more valued than two-bedroom homes because more families and even couples want the extra space. Likewise, having two bathrooms is a big plus over one bathroom.

Heads up: An older three-bedroom one-story may not be comparable with a new, three-bedroom two story, even if they are on the same street.

4. **Condition.** Even if you think your home is in good condition, look again. Buyers will consider the following: Are the appliances new? How old are the roof, heating and air system, carpet, and paint? How well are the other homes in the neighborhood maintained?

Cost per square foot

Cost per square foot is the second most commonly used method to determine property value. It's used to compare properties that have a number of differences or for properties being sold at different prices.

To calculate your cost per square foot, divide the asking price of your house by the number of square feet:

Price/Square Feet

A three-bedroom home with 1,200 square feet might be worth more than a two-bedroom home with 1,300 square feet.

Example: If your asking price is $100,000 and your home has 1,200 square feet, divide $100,000 by 1,200. The answer is the cost of your house per square foot—$83.33.

The cost per square foot on a one story may be higher than on a two story with the same square footage. The reason is that a two-story home can have the same square footage on a much smaller lot. The difference in price is the difference in land value.

The cost per square foot on a one story may be higher than on a two story with the same square footage.

Additional factors to consider

There are other factors to consider that can affect the value of your home, but generally these are less important than location, size, and number of bedrooms and bathrooms. Some of these will be more difficult to calculate unless you use a specialist. When looking through local comps, there are a number of additional things to compare:

1. **Distance.** The best comps are located within a quarter-mile radius of your property. If you are in an area with little market activity or in a rural area, using comparable properties from farther away may be necessary.

2. **Date of sale of comp**. Appraisers prefer recent home sales (ones that have taken place within the last six months). If the market is slow, they may need to go back twelve months.

3. **Construction**. Brick, wood, vinyl siding, etc.

4. **Condition.** Even when everything else is the same, obviously a house in poor condition will have a lower value than one that has been kept up.

5. **Age.** Where possible, use comps that are the same age as your property. Try to stay within three years difference, either older or younger. By the way, a rehabbed property does not hold the same value as a new one.

6. **Square footage**. Square footage is determined by the amount of heated square feet. Try to keep your comps

within 100 square feet. Unheated basements and garages do not count in square footage.

> *Unheated basements and garages do not count in square footage.*

7. **Number of floors**. Use properties that have the same number as your property.

8. **Basement**. If your house is on a crawl space or slab, use comps on crawl spaces or slabs. If you have a basement, pull comps with basements. Try to keep the square footage of the basements as close as possible.

The value of some housing features varies depending upon the region of the country. Basements often come with homes in the North where the freeze line is deep so the foundations, or basements, are as well. In warmer climates the freeze line, if there is any, is very shallow, so all that is required for the foundation is a crawl space under the house. Some Southern homes are built directly on top of concrete slabs and have no crawl space.

> *Basements often come with homes in the North where the freeze line is deep so the foundations, or basements, are also.*

9. **Garage or carport**. Again, use same for same.

10. **Lot size**. Compare similar size lots.

11. **How long has the property been on the market?** A long time on the market may indicate that it's overpriced. A buyer will typically assume (1) you are now an eager seller or (2) you have set an unrealistic sales price and aren't willing to work with offers.

12. Why are you selling? A buyer may want to know because, for example, if you have been transferred and are moving soon, you are most likely motivated. If you are not willing to move without a high enough offer, you are not seen as motivated. And, if you're extremely motivated you may be willing to offer owner financing as discussed in Chapter 7.

You get the idea. The more similarities between properties, the easier it will be for agents and buyers to comp your property. It is often very difficult to find like-kind comparisons. When comps vary significantly from your property, they are not really comps! Numbers need to be adjusted accordingly and this takes experience and training. If it were easy, we wouldn't need agents or appraisers!

Pricing is important

Investigate your competition before you decide on your listing price. You may even consider getting a professional appraiser's value before setting your price. Appraisals are less biased and more accurate than a broker's price opinion (BPO) from your agent. And, it will help you know whether, once you have an offer, the bank's appraiser will agree with your asking price.

> *Houses get the most attention the first two to six weeks they are on the market.*

Studies show that pricing too far outside the area's price range can actually slow down the sale. Too high is never good and too low makes buyers think something is wrong with the property. This is another reason to do your due diligence when comping. Be sure to price accurately from the beginning.

Houses get the most attention the first two to six weeks they are on the market. Automated search programs sort through new listings and e-mail them to buyer lists. Buyers constantly search for new listings. And, if you house doesn't sell, buyers, agents, and neighbors question what's wrong with your property.

In summary

Your property "fair market value" is determined by looking at and comparing recent sale prices of similar properties in the area. When determining value, compare prices of properties that have sold rather than using properties that are still listed for sale, as most homes sell for less than the listed price.

A great way to begin learning true value is to search real estate listings and visit open houses in your area. This will help you get a feel for local pricing. When visiting open houses, go to ones that are more expensive and less expensive than your property. The more you see, the more you will begin to understand what your property is worth and what value things like a bedroom or bathroom add.

There is a lot of property information available with the click of a mouse. Find everything you need to know before you set your price.

In today's real estate market, plan to be patient and don't be surprised if you have to lower your asking price. Price is the key. If your house isn't selling, you could be asking too much.

Chapter 15

MARKETING— HOW EFFECTIVE IS YOURS?

N eed buyers? When trying to sell your house, the answer is a resounding "yes!" If you don't understand marketing, it could be the reason you're not reaching your audience.

Should you market your property?

You know my answer. Even when using an agent, many simply put your property on the MLS, place a sign in the yard, and move on to their next property. They have to stay busy with other clients while waiting for your house to sell or how will they eat?

So, yes, market your property. This will not eliminate the need for your real estate agent; this will help bring buyers in the door to get your property sold.

Besides, no one knows your home better than you, so who do you think will market more passionately?

Do buyers know your house is for sale?

They'd better! Here are some ways to make sure they do:

- **Yard sign**—Is there a sign in the yard? With a phone number *that someone answers* and a website that is monitored regularly? Is it easy to read when driving by?

- **Flyer Box**—Do you have the property information available in a flyer box in front of the house? Flyer boxes market anytime someone drives by.

- **MLS**—Is your property listed on the multiple listing service with fabulous photos and an outstanding description of the most desirable features? Even if you're selling on your own (For Sale By Owner), there are agents or companies who will do a flat fee listing, only charging you to put the property on the MLS.

- **Newspaper ads**—Is it in a newspaper ad that stands out from the others?

- **Online listing sites**—Is it on the free online listing sites (and there are a TON of them)?

- **Neighbors**—Have you put out flyers, talked to your neighbors and co-workers about your house? Neighbors are a huge source of referrals.

- **Finder's gift**—Have you offered a finder's gift if someone refers the person who buys your home (i.e., $250, a gift card, a microwave, a flat screen TV)?

- **Don't blend in**— What have you done above and beyond the

Being pro-active is absolutely necessary to find a qualified buyer. Good news, it's easier than ever today with all the available online help.

usual that makes your property get attention? Why would someone find you in the stack of homes for sale?

Tips for effective marketing

- **Headlines**—You *must* stand out. The entire goal of your headline/title is to grab attention. Notice which ads grab your attention. Which ones do you open and read? Why?

- **Unique pricing**—Use digits other than "000" or "900" to increase interest. One idea is to use the digits of your address. For example, if your address is 368 Main Street and the value is $150,000, make your price $150,368. The unusual number jumps out as buyers read the ads. We always use the number "7" instead of the number "9" because it's less familiar.

- **Don't forget benefits**—Most sellers list "features" (number of bedrooms and baths) but leave out "benefits" (close to shopping and dining, close to (list major highways), list the desirable schools, etc.).

- **Photos**—Always include the maximum number allowed. Buyers want to see lots of pictures so make sure you have plenty and that they're crisp and clear.

- **Videos**—I recently bought a flip camera for less than $100 and a wide angle lens for another $50. It was well worth the investment. More and more sellers and agents are using videos and buyers want to see room layouts as they walk through the space via video. Can't do them yourself? Find a friend who will do them for you.

- **Craigslist**—Free and available all over the country. Read other ads for ideas—see which ones stand out to you and why. Be sure to add the maximum number of photos. You'll need to update your ad on Craigslist every two to three days as they quickly fall down the list of newly placed properties but this is one of the most frequented sites and it's FREE!

- **Newspapers**—We find newspapers to be expensive and fairly ineffective. It's hard to make your property stand out from the crowd in a newspaper. And a huge portion of the population no longer reads newspapers. There are many more effective and less expensive ways to market your home.

> *Make sure all of your marketing has your contact information.*

- **Contact information**—Make sure all of your marketing has your contact information, another tip that seems obvious. However, I've picked up more than one marketing flyer from an information box only to later realize that it had the property address but no way to contact an agent or seller.

Be sure *all* marketing includes:

1. The property address

2. Photos

3. Description details (i.e., number of bedrooms and baths, square footage)

4. Benefits (i.e., schools, shopping, etc.)

5. A contact name, phone number and e-mail address

Marketing ideas I use:

1. **Lighted signage**—Use signage that's illuminated even after dark.

2. **Take-aways**—At open house, hand out something your lookers will remember, something that will be a positive reminder of your home. Hand out bottles of water, flyers

> *Coupons for local merchants are a great give-away and help prospects learn what's available nearby.*

about your property and any local information you can provide. Coupons for local merchants are a great give-away and help prospects learn what's available nearby. I do seasonal gifts. In the spring, I'll have packets of herb seeds or small herb plants to hand out. Walk through Dollar Stores to find inexpensive, seasonal hand-out ideas.

3. **Informational flyer**—Create a flyer with all the local conveniences you can find: shopping, schools, universities, hospitals, malls, restaurants, gas stations, attractions in the area, local police and fire stations, even school bus pick up locations. Assume your lookers don't know the neighborhood.

4. **Comparable info**—Hand out comp information on your home as well as information on the other listed properties in the area showing that your house is the best value.

5. **Staging**—Do some staging to make sure your home looks its best. Springtime is easy—sit out potted plants, have lemons and limes in bowls or in vases. Make it feel like springtime—light, airy, and fun! During the holidays, decorate sparingly and try not to make it religion specific, which may turn off some buyers. Setting out fresh flowers and candles adds warmth and charm. The point of staging is to have buyers think, "wow!"

6. **Incentives**—Offer any and all you can think of!

   ■ Pay for a free session with a landscape architect

   ■ Offer $1,000 landscape allowance

   ■ Pay homeowners fees for a year

- Offer $1,000 for new appliances or any home improvement; let buyers spend it on what they choose

- Offer a new carpet or flooring allowance; let buyers pick their own

- Gift certificates to Lowes or Home Depot

- Give free lawn service for a year

- Throw in a home warranty

- Offer to pay closing costs

- Be creative!

7. **Voicemail**—When selling your house yourself, be available! Consider adding a phone number to your family plan that you can use in your marketing. Or, if you plan to use your existing phone number, be sure to add a voicemail message with property information and assurance that you will get back to the caller as soon as possible.

8. **Owner financing**—Offer owner financing (discussed in Chapter 7) or to carry back a second mortgage for the amount they can't borrow.

> *I mail an average of 250–450 letters to surrounding homes telling neighbors the day and time of the open house and that we pay gifts for finding our buyer.*

9. **Neighborhood letters**—Send letters to the neighbors inviting them to "pick their neighbor" with information about your home and the open house. Give them an incentive to talk about it to others (i.e., $200 gift card if they find your buyer). I mail an average of 250–450 letters to

surrounding homes telling neighbors the day and time of the open house and that we pay gifts for finding our buyer.

10. **Signs**—Not just signs in the yard, but as many directional signs to your home as the neighborhood allows. Make it easy for passersby to find your home.

11. **Flyers**—Put them out in surrounding shopping areas.

12. **Virtual tour**—Video your home and put the virtual tour online.

13. **Market your home's advantages**—Great schools, low crime, convenient to parks, major highways, great shopping, spectacular views, easy access to local attractions—any you can think of!

14. **Description**—The words you use to describe your property are *very* important. Words such as "move-in ready," "gorgeous," "beautiful," and "landscaping" really help! "Motivated" or "must sell," statistics show, actually slow down sales.

15. **Human resource departments**—E-mail HR departments at local companies. Many employees prefer to live close to their jobs and many employers prefer it as well. Make it easy for them to find yours!

16. **Make your house sing!** - Whatever you have, paint it, clean it, fix it, make sure it works properly and looks great. That includes the yard, the exterior, and the interior. Don't forget the attic and crawl space. Buyers have options, make yours stand out.

17. **Price aggressively (low)**—Start as low as you can. Buyers are still going to ask for, and expect, reductions, and they will also expect that anything in your home that isn't perfect be fixed.

18. **Re-price**—Be prepared to lower your asking price every four to six weeks. When you lower your price, make it significant.

If you make small drops, they'll wait for more. Significant drops make buyers eager to rush in ahead of others.

19. **Pay closing costs**—It's more and more common for sellers to offer this to attract buyers.

Remember, you may take a hit when you sell but, when you buy, you get all the benefits you forfeit when you sell. You'll be able to buy at a discount for the same reasons you're selling at one.

Did you know?

According to the National Association of Realtors, single women make up approximately 20 percent of all homebuyers while single men account for only 12 percent.

Their study showed three main reasons single women are buying homes in record numbers: to relocate closer to work or family, because they need more space, and the No. 1 reason is... that nurturing female instinct, a strong desire to nest.

Women make better salaries than previous generations. They understand the need for creating their own security and, divorce rates being what they are, no longer sit back hoping someone else will provide for them. Later in their careers, divorced women and female retirees are downsizing on their own.

When selling, the fact that single women account for one-fifth of all buyers is a valuable number to have. In sales, it's critical to know your target audience and craft your product to meet their needs. Have you noticed automobiles with flower holders built into the dash? The automotive industry studies who their buyers are and so should you.

Armed with this information, will your marketing strategy change?

Chapter 16

HOW TO HAVE AN OPEN HOUSE

I f you want to sell, buyers need to see the inside. An open house is a great way to get a number through on the same day, which creates energy and buzz.

I have open house on Sundays from 2 p.m. to 4 p.m. In our area, that's when most real estate agents have their open houses so that's when the public is out looking for them. Make use of your local agents' marketing.

There are a number of reasons to have an open house. One, of course, is to show off the property. You're able to show your home to people who are interested in the neighborhood. You're also able to show it to the neighbors, who are always curious, and who may know someone wanting to live there.

Neighbors are always interested in who will be moving in, so give them the opportunity to pick their neighbors!

Getting prepared

For any house showing, have your home's best face ready! Even if you're not putting it on the market for another month, now is the time to be getting it ready.

Here are some things you need to do:

1. **Clear out the clutter!** Clean out cabinets and closets. Throw out what you can; give away what can be passed on; box up what you want to keep that's out of season and you won't be using for a while. This gives a more open and airy feeling for buyers who will be coming through. It also gets you closer to being ready to move!

2. **Clean up the yard.** Get rid of all debris—anything dead or dying. Rake the yard well and throw out new seed. Freshen up flower beds with bark or straw and plant flowering plants when the weather allows. Cut back overgrowth.

3. **Exterior touch up.** Make sure the front door looks fresh and the hardware is in good, functioning order. No loose or difficult door knobs.

4. **Interior touch up.** Clean carpets as needed. Clean moldings and switch plate covers. Sticky fingerprints from your little ones are not attractive to potential buyers. Make sure window treatments hang straight and replace any damaged blinds. Anything your looker notices as not right drops their offer and is seen by them as more work once they move in.

5. **Make sure the kitchen and bathrooms sparkle!** (Just like you want in the property you're buying.) Let the buyer see the joy of living in the home. You don't want them focused on anything negative or anything that looks like work needing to be done.

6. **Pets**—I know this is a touchy subject and I understand. However, many buyers are not interested in seeing your pet, your pet's household objects, or the lingering smell that your pet may have left in the home. To make your home

If your home is "ready to sell," your buyer will be more impressed, their offer will be higher, and you're so much closer to being able to move!

ready to show to the buying public and increase your chance of a sale, it's best to remove all evidence of your pet for any showings including open house.

It's always worth the effort. If your home is "ready to sell," your buyer will be more impressed, their offer will be higher, and you're so much closer to being able to move!

How to have an open house

Yes, you should have an open house. But don't just put a sign in the yard and leave the door open. To be successful, there must be some preparation.

1. **Advertise—a lot.** Post notices of open house on the MLS, Craigslist, Postlets (which feeds to multiple websites), Zillow, Trulia, etc. Anywhere your house is listed, change the ad to include Open House, the date, and times. If possible, advertise in neighborhood newsletters and websites.

2. **Mail a neighborhood letter** the week of open house letting the neighbors know that the house is now ready for sale and inviting them to come by and take a look. Point out that this is a great time for them to "pick their neighbor."

   I send out, on average, 250–450 letters to surrounding homes telling neighbors the day and time of the open house and that we give referral gifts to anyone finding our buyer.

3. **Directional open house signs**, not just the sign in the yard, but directional arrows throughout the neighborhood so passersby know there's an open house and how to find it. Be sure to have plenty posted and well positioned from every neighborhood entry point. This is especially important if your home is near the back of the neighborhood.

   A number of neighborhoods, especially the newer ones, have sign ordinances. One area where we own many homes only allows open house and directional signs from Friday afternoon to Monday morning. So, that's when I put out all the directional arrow signs and the open house sign in the front yard. The morning of the open house, tie balloons to the signs so they can't be missed. Don't forget to pick up the signs when open house is over.

4. **Have the home and yard neat and tidy.** Even if you're leaving some of the fix up for the next owners, the house and yard should be tidied up. You don't want prospects feeling overwhelmed when they see lots of clean up and repairs needing to be done.

5. **Turn on all the lights** (make sure all the bulbs work) so the house looks bright and cheery. Open all blinds to let in natural light and expand the rooms with exterior views. Turn on ALL lights in the house including closets, under cabinet and stove vent lighting. I place candles around for a pleasant scent (I prefer vanilla) and some accent, especially in the bathrooms. Candles also look beautiful in a fireplace.

6. **Have a sign-in sheet.** Ask for name, e-mail address, and phone number. Always follow up the next day to thank visitors for coming by, to see what they thought of the house, and to find out if they have additional questions. Follow-up is very important and something most sellers or agents don't do. Visitors can be a great source of information for things you should improve before the next prospect comes through.

7. **Have a hand-out sheet** that includes a photo of the home (so they remember which house it's from when they leave) and as many of the positive features as you can list. Many buyers will look at more than one house in the same day and can forget yours in a very short time without a photo and information sheet. Get flyers out of information tubes from homes that are for sale to use as your examples, and then improve upon them!

8. **Smell/odor/aroma**—Air out your home so it doesn't smell stuffy, like animals or like last night's dinner! Some people

suggest baking and handing out cookies so the house smells good and homey. Others suggest you bake them for aroma but hide them away. Cookies cause crumbs and some people may be allergic to ingredients, so beware of this idea!

9.   **Hand-outs**—I prefer to hand out bottled water and a small, non-edible gift to lookers. Guests are always pleased with take-aways. They leave with a positive impression of the home and remember yours above the others simply because you had treats!

> *Keep your open house simple so you're fresh and excited about it.*

10. **What time to hold an open house.** I hold open house on Sunday from 2 p.m. to 4 p.m. because that's standard in our area for real estate agent open houses. Most of the public is trained to be out at those hours looking for open houses so I want to capture that already existing viewer. I have done the same hours on Saturday when the property is located in a high traffic area and I can be assured of good turnout even without advertising ahead of time. My Saturday marketing is simply directional signs and balloons.

11. **FYI:** Make sure you have toilet paper in the house. This is an important note if your house is vacant. I don't think I've had an open house where no one used the restroom!

Should you be present at open house?

If you're selling your home yourself, yes, you need to be there to show the property and answer questions. If you have a contract with a real estate agent to market the property for you, they should be present at open house and it is better if you are not.

Why? Because the agent is doing the negotiating for you and putting a buffer between you and the buyer. Also, if potential buyers know you are there, they naturally feel uncomfortable and will not speak truthfully about how they feel about the house.

Plus, lookers tend to make a hasty exit and not spend the time they should in a home when the seller is present.

Last, but not least, if you hear negative comments about your home, your natural tendency will be to defend (like "That brass hardware is the best money can buy!"). Better to have a third party between you and your buyer to smooth any places that may need negotiating.

The day of open house, make plans to be somewhere else.

Finally

Keep your open house simple so you're fresh and excited about it. Your enthusiasm for the home helps to sell it. Not everyone will have positive things to say but, remember, it only takes one person who loves it to get it sold.

Good luck with your selling. Open houses work.

Section Five

THE SALES PROCESS

- Should you hire a real estate agent?

- Is your buyer qualified?

- How do you handle an offer and your counter offers?

- What can you expect from a home inspection?

- What are closing costs and what will you be expected to pay?

Follow along; this is going to be a great section!

Chapter 17

HIRING A REAL ESTATE AGENT

Using a real estate agent when selling a home is not required. Many sellers start their process by putting a for-sale-by-owner sign in the yard.

Do you know how to handle the process on your own? And what will being listed with an agent do for bringing in buyers?

When selling without an agent, a real estate attorney or title company handles the paperwork and closing process. They provide assistance and guidance once you find a willing buyer and reach an agreement to purchase.

If you don't hire an agent to list your property, you could still end up paying commission to the buyer's agent. If six percent commission is the going rate in your area, be prepared to pay three percent to any agent who brings a willing and able buyer to your door.

> *Using a real estate agent when selling a home is not required.*

How do you decide which agent to hire?

There are more than 1.2 million Realtors in the United States, and that number doesn't include real estate agents who are not members of the National Association of Realtors.

By the way, a Realtor and a real estate agent are not necessarily the same thing. They are both licensed to sell real estate. A Realtor, however, belongs to the National Association of Realtors and must abide by their code of ethics. A real estate agent does not. So, a Realtor is a real estate agent, but not all real estate agents are Realtors.

Questions to ask potential agents:

1. How long have you been in the real estate business?

2. Do you work in real estate full-time?

3. Do you have an assistant? Are they licensed?

4. What are your working hours?

5. What is your preferred means of communication (e-mail, phone, text, fax)?

6. Will you be available during this entire process?

7. Has anyone ever sued you over a real estate transaction? What was the outcome?

8. Have you ever had an ethics complaint to the local Realtor board or the state department of real estate? What was the outcome?

9. Do you have errors-and-omission insurance to protect against any mistakes you or your assistant(s) might make?

10. How many clients did you work with last year? How many completed a transaction with you?

11. May I have references of people who have bought or sold property with your help?

12. What marketing strategies will you use to help sell my property?

13. Are you familiar with my specific area?

14. How will you help me negotiate the best possible price and terms?

15. Will you handle coordinating inspections, repairs, and closing documents?

16. Will you be at the closing?

It would also be good to ask the prospective agent if they're familiar with some of the creative selling solutions you've learned here like owner financing and lease option.

Don't be intimidated when doing a thorough interview. Professionals expect it and also prefer to interview you as a client.

When selling, often things such as time frames, repairs, or values of personal property need to be negotiated. Your agent should be able to comfortably lead you through these negotiations as well.

An agent insulates you from direct negotiations

Don't take hiring an agent lightly. You need someone capable, professional and with whom you can communicate comfortably over the long haul.

with the buyer. This can be good to keep emotions calm, but sometimes inability to communicate directly with the buyer can be frustrating.

So, don't take hiring an agent lightly. Selling your home will be a very lengthy and important process. You need someone capable, professional, and with whom you can communicate comfortably over the long haul.

There is much more to buying and selling a home than the sales price. If you decide to hire an agent, find an experienced one who knows what to do to lead both parties to a swift and agreeable closing.

Different types of agency

Agents perform a variety of roles, so if you hire one, know your options and what you're hiring.

- **Listing agent**—The listing agent is actually the real estate company itself. The individual agent who lists and markets the property is known as the "sub-agent" of the listing agent. In fact, all agents working for the listing real estate company are sub-agents. Agents have added financial incentive to sell any "in-house" properties, which are properties listed by anyone in their company office.

- **Buyer's agent**—Works on behalf of the buyer. Discloses all details of the transaction to the buyer.

- **Seller's agent**—Works on behalf of the seller. Discloses all details of the transaction to the seller.

- **Dual agent**—An agent working with a buyer who wants to purchase a listing held by the agent or the agent's firm. A dual agent must be loyal to both the buyer and the seller.

- **Designated agent**—Similar to a dual agent. The broker-in-charge designates one agent to represent the buyer and one agent to represent the seller.

Best way to find an agent

Recommendations. Whom do you know and what was their experience with their agent? Interview multiple agents and various real estate companies. Continue the process until you find one who best suits your needs. You will be in a close, personal relationship with this agent for months and need to make sure you can work with him or her, communicate openly, and trust him or her as a professional to lead you through the entire process. You want a hardworking, results-driven agent with whom you have rapport to make the process as easy as possible.

If you decide to work with an agent, be sure to ask if they are working for you or for the buyer, and ask them to keep all of your conversations confidential.

Your goal, and that of your agent, should be open, comfortable communication and a swift, successful closing.

Agreeing with your agent on an asking price

This is where you'll want to be sure you've done your due diligence. Just because your neighbor, your relative, or a real estate agent says you should list at a certain price doesn't mean this person is correct. Do your homework as discussed in Chapter 14, Determining Your Property Value, to know all you can about your market and to come up with your own estimate of the fair market value.

Many sellers list with the agent who promises the highest selling price for the home. This is unfortunate, because some agents inflate their first suggested price just to get the listing. Those agents are not helping when they make you think your house is worth more than it is.

Any sign in your yard initiates sales calls to your agent, even if not for your house. Once you've signed a contract, the agent who listed your house at an inflated price hopes you'll lower it in the future to a point where it will sell. The ultimate responsibility and benefit for getting the house sold, however, is yours.

The ultimate responsibility and benefit for getting the house sold is yours.

How much is real estate commission?

The norm in most states is six percent real estate commission: three percent to the listing agent and three percent to the selling agent. Check your area—the amount can vary depending not just on your state but also on location such as mountain or waterfront properties.

Commission will be a cost when selling your property, so factor it into your expenses. You will pay it to your listing agent as well as to any real estate agent who brings a buyer. Real estate commission will be shown as a deduction on your side (seller) of the HUD-1. If you sell the home yourself as a for-sale-by-owner, you will not have to pay a listing agent, but you will be expected to pay any agent who ultimately brings your buyer.

Commission will be a cost when selling your property, so factor it into your expenses.

Can you fire an agent if you don't like him or her?

Suppose you get into a contract with an agent and weeks, or months, down the line, you are not happy with this person or the service provided. Do you have to stay with this agent until the end of the contract?

I asked our agents this question and they assured me that, yes, you can get out of a contract with a non-performing agent. You'll need to write something to the company explaining why you want to terminate the contract as they don't want you to cancel for something unethical on your part, like trying to sell to someone who's already viewed the property without paying the agent commission.

If the reasons are valid, however, the company certainly should let you terminate the contract. Valid reasons would include no communication, no perceivable marketing, or the agent doing something wrong or unethical.

For this reason, many sellers don't want to sign a long listing agreement. It's hard to know, going in, if the agent will really work well for you. Most agents prefer to sign a year listing agreement but many sellers opt for as short as three months. Length of contract, like so many things in the real estate transaction, is negotiable.

Length of the listing contract, like so many things in the real estate transaction, is negotiable.

The contract works both ways, of course. Give your agent a fair price to work with, have the property available any time a prospect wants to see it, and give your agent the necessary time to get it sold before you get frustrated with his or her efforts.

Chapter 18

IS YOUR BUYER QUALIFIED?

There is no sense wasting time showing your home and accepting an offer from a prospect who can never close on your property. The question is, how do you know?

To begin with, ask! "Are you pre-approved? Show me your letter of proof."

Be sure you receive the buyer's lender qualification letter before you consider an offer. Or, if you accept without proof of a pre-approval, know that this person may not qualify for a loan or perhaps not qualify for your price range. It's risky to take your home off the market without some assurance of a buyer's ability to qualify to buy.

Know how much your buyer can borrow

Before most real estate agents will work with buyers, and before you take any offer seriously, make

It's risky to take your home off the market without some assurance of a buyer's ability to qualify to buy.

sure the buyer has talked with a lender and received either a pre-qualification letter or a pre-approval for a loan.

Pre-qualification

A pre-qualification amount is an estimate that gives the buyer an idea of what he or she can afford to purchase. It is not a guaranteed amount that a lender will approve.

A pre-qualification is relatively easy to obtain, but not very valuable. It is a quick evaluation of creditworthiness used to determine the *estimated* amount the buyer can afford to borrow.

To pre-qualify, a loan officer will take some of their information (employment, income, assets, current debt) and make an estimate of the borrowing range they should be able to repay to a lender. The loan officer *will not verify any of it.*

A pre-qualification can be done over the phone and without filling out any paperwork. With most pre-qualifications, no social security number is taken so there is no credit check.

Letter of Pre-Qualification for Loan Application

December 20, 2011

Borrower: Mr. & Mrs. Smith

Borrower Address: 123 Main Street, Greensboro, NC 27410

Pre-Qualified for purchase of property at the following address:
    789 Dream Street, Greensboro, NC 27410

Pre-Qualification is based on ownership as:
    ☒ 1) Primary Residence   ☐ 2) Investment Property   ☐ 3) Second Home

Dear: Mr. & Mrs. Smith

After review of the financial information provided by you and a review of your current credit report, we feel that you are preliminarily qualified based on the affordability, credit and terms you have requested. All of the above is subject to the standard underwriting guidelines of Benchmark Mortgage and any other underwriting investor or agency involved.

This letter is not a commitment to lend funds, but is for pre-qualification purposes only. A loan decision can only be made after completion of a comprehensive underwriting review of the information contained in the Uniform Residential Loan Application for the appropriate loan program.

_____

Lender

Pre-approval

A pre-approval determines whether a buyer can qualify for a loan and the maximum amount the lender would be willing to lend them.

The process of pre-approval involves a *thorough* look into income and expenses, a look at both credit report and score, and a *confirmation* of income. The buyer will be asked to submit their social security number.

A pre-approved mortgage must still be reviewed once the buyer finds a specific property. The specific dollar amount in the pre-approval is not guaranteed.

However, as long as no major income or credit changes occur between the time of pre-approval and the actual purchase of a home, the dollar amount of the pre-approval should be good.

When an offer is presented with a pre-approval letter, you know the buyers have already taken steps to qualify to buy your house. Again, a pre-approval letter from a lender is *not* a guarantee that the loan will be provided, but why start the process without knowing that your buyer is qualified?

Letter of Conditional Approval of your Loan Application

December 20, 2011

Borrower: Mr. & Mrs. Smith
Borrower **Address:** 123 Main Street, Greensboro, NC 27410

Pre-Approved for purchase of property at the following address:
     789 Dream Street, Greensboro, NC 27410

Pre-Approval on this property is based on ownership as:
     __X__ 1) Primary Residence _____2) Investment Property _____3) Second Home

Dear Mr. & Mrs. Smith

Congratulations! We are delighted to inform you that after review of your financial information and completion of an underwriting analysis, Benchmark Mortgage has conditionally approved your mortgage loan request. Following is a summary of key loan terms to which this approval applies:

This pre-approval is subject to but not limited to the following other conditions being satisfied:
*   Acceptable contract of sale on suitable property
*   No material changes have occurred in applicant's financial condition, creditworthiness, or purpose for the loan prior to closing.
*   All closing conditions of Lender and/or Investor must be satisfied including but not limited to: clear transfer of title, acceptable and adequate title insurance, acceptable hazard insurance, flood certification, any/all inspections according to real estate contract.
*   Acceptable review of appraisal of subject property
*   Satisfaction of any and all investor closing conditions

This approval letter is subject to your acceptance of the terms, and the conditions stated herein as being fully satisfied prior to closing.

This pre-approval is not a commitment to lend funds, but a conditional approval of your loan application and all the conditions listed above are subject to final underwriting and final investor approval.

If you have any questions regarding the conditions or terms of this approval, please feel free to contact us.

Sincerely,

_____

Lender

Chapter 19

THE OFFER

O nce you've arrived at this point, you've found a buyer who's willing and able to purchase your home. How exciting! New questions: What's too much? What's too little? What's just right? Let's break down the different aspects of offers and counter offers.

What's the right amount?

In a depressed real estate market, you shouldn't expect a full price offer. In recent years, offers nationally averaged 3 percent to 5 percent below asking price. Experts say the average national discount below the asking price today is about 7 percent. Don't be surprised when the offer is less than you're asking.

On the other hand, what if they offer more than you're asking? Rare today but, yes, sometimes a bidding war happens and buyers offer more than the asking price. If this happens to you, consider if your home will appraise for that higher amount.

Before receiving offers, make sure you've already done your homework and determined (1) your property's fair market value and (2) the lowest amount you can accept for it. Use the information you gained when determining your selling price (discussed in Chapter 14) to help both you and the buyer come to an agreement about what the home is worth.

Besides the mortgage, buyers know they will incur additional costs with the purchase including inspections, taxes, repairs, and necessary updates when they move in. There are more costs to buying than just the purchase price itself. It's common for the buyer to ask you, the seller, to pay some of these costs. You can agree to pay some outright or show that you've already provided for them by agreeing to lower your asking price.

> *Knowing your numbers is absolutely necessary before receiving an offer so you know exactly how much you can negotiate away.*

Knowing your numbers is absolutely necessary before receiving an offer so you know exactly how much you can negotiate away.

Everything's negotiable!

Many times buyers see something in the house that they want the sellers to leave. It's very possible they'll ask for these items in their offer. Items that are often part of the negotiation include appliances, window treatments, light fixtures, furnishings, yard equipment such as lawn mowers, sheds, and even plants and pots on the deck. Sometimes these items are what made the buyer fall in love with your home. Think through ahead of time which items you are willing to throw in as part of the negotiation.

When I purchased a for-sale-by-owner house to live in myself, the husband was out of town the night I went over to sign the purchase and sale agreement. I asked for, and the wife eagerly threw in, all the appliances (including washer and dryer). It may have been because she wanted new ones with her new home, but her husband was not thrilled when he found out! Make sure you're on the same page with everyone involved in the sale of the property about what you can negotiate away.

To make the purchase of their home attractive to buyers, many sellers are paying some, or even all, of the closing costs. Don't be surprised if your buyer makes this request in their offer.

With all these variables, you can see why it's important to plan ahead what you can spend, what you can leave and, after all the negotiations, what your bottom line must be.

How much earnest money should you expect?

To make the purchase of their home attractive to buyers, many sellers are paying some, or even all, of the closing costs.

Earnest money is a deposit given when an offer is placed. It shows that the buyer is serious about purchasing your home. Typically, earnest money is 1 percent to 5 percent of the offer. The less the buyer puts down, the less they risk losing if they back out of the deal. The more the buyer puts down, the more serious you may consider their offer.

When you accept an offer, the earnest money becomes part of the buyer's down payment. If you reject the offer, the earnest money is returned to the buyer. If the buyer backs out of the deal, depending upon the circumstances, they may forfeit the earnest money deposit and it becomes money to you for having your home off the market during the time their offer was considered.

When you accept an offer, the earnest money becomes part of the buyer's down payment.

What is a home warranty?

Most buyers now require the seller to provide a good home warranty. Cost is typically $350–$500, and the warranty service contract will cover things like the repair or replacement of appliances and heating and air systems if they break down in the first year of homeownership.

What is an appliance allowance?

Are your appliances dated? Rather than replacing them, many sellers give an allowance (for example, $1,000) toward replacement, allowing the buyer to purchase his or her own appliances after closing.

Offers

Be open. Don't be offended by low offers. Always consider every offer because you never know which one is going to lead to the sale. A lower offer from a qualified buyer is better than a higher offer from someone who will not qualify for financing. And, a lower offer may turn out to be a better deal than a higher offer with a lot of contingencies (conditions). Look at the entire offer, not just the offer price.

> *Don't be offended by low offers. Consider every offer because you never know which one is going to lead to the sale.*

Contingencies

A contingency in a real estate contract is a provision that specifies the contract will cease to exist if a certain event occurs. For example: "This contract is contingent upon the buyer obtaining a mortgage loan at an interest rate of 6 percent or lower." If this rate is not available or the buyer is not able to qualify for this rate or lower, the contract ends.

There are many common contingencies that may occur in your contract. Some of the more common contingencies include:

- **Financing contingency**—As in the example above, the buyer will be able to obtain X amount at X interest rate by X date, or the contract ends.

- **Appraisal contingency**—Most contracts have a contingency clause stating that the property must appraise for or above the agreed selling price.

- **Inspection contingency**—States that the necessary repairs found during a formal inspection cannot exceed a certain dollar amount or the contract may be terminated.

As with everything else in the contract, contingencies are open to negotiation. If, for example, the property does not appraise high enough to meet the agreed-to sales price, the seller can lower his or her price. If the needed repairs exceed the specified amount, the seller can lower the asking price, offer to pay to have the repairs done, or the buyer can waive the contingency, etc.

Counter offers

When you finally receive an offer, you have three options: accept, reject, or counter.

If the offer is extremely low, don't be offended. The seller maybe hopeful, may be anticipating a great "deal" like they've heard about from the media, or may actually turn out to be the one who does buy your home. You never know. So, it's best to be receptive and respond with thought and sincerity.

Most buyers offer expecting you to respond with a counter somewhere in the middle. Some are really interested in your home but it is more than they can afford so the offer is hopeful on their part.

How to respond with a counter

You are not required to respond after receiving an offer. Typically, the offer states a time frame for your response, after which the offer automatically expires. Most often, rather than accepting or rejecting the first offer, you will instead make a counter offer.

You are presented with an offer. You respond with a counter offer because the offer was unacceptable. Your counter revises the initial offer. Responding with a counter offer is a way to decline a previous offer while continuing negotiations.

Counter offers are a normal part of the buying and selling process. A counter is perfectly acceptable. The counter offer is where the negotiations really begin and you can start to understand the strength of the buyer's interest in your home.

You may counter with a higher price, and/or you may change some of the terms of the offer. Other than price negotiation, you may ask for a higher down payment, request an earlier closing date, refuse to leave the appliances, etc. Counter offers are considered new offers and the process starts over with each new counter.

The buyer may accept or they may make adjustments and counter your counter offer, (making theirs a second counter offer, or counter offer No. 2). There is no limit to the number of counter offers that can go back and forth. As with the original offer, no response is required to a counter, so each contains an expiration time just like the original offer to purchase.

> *Counter offers are considered new offers and the process starts over with each new counter.*

A counter offer is not an outright rejection of an offer. You and the buyer are continuing the negotiations, which is good! The goal is to keep the counter offers going because, as soon as one of you stops countering without an acceptance, the deal is dead.

Typical response time for an offer or counter offer is twenty-four hours. If you make a counter offer and change your mind, you can back out. You are allowed to withdraw your counter as long as the buyer has not yet accepted. Once an acceptance is communicated to you or your agent, and/or to the buyer or the buyer's agent, you have a contract.

You never have to accept an offer. If you do not agree with what they are requiring from you as the seller, you are within your rights to end the negotiations.

Agents must present to you any legal offer made in writing that is accompanied by a deposit check. An agent can never refuse to present an offer because he or she feels it is too low. If you receive an offer that you find offensive, you can choose to simply end the negotiations.

Always prepare for an inspection

Unless your house is being sold "as is," most offers are contingent upon an inspection. This means that if the buyer does not approve after inspection, the deal is dead and he or she gets the earnest money back. Allow the inspection to be completed as quickly as possible so both you and the buyer know whether you have a completed contract. Two weeks is a good time frame to allow.

The buyer will receive a written copy of the findings and may request any or all of the items repaired. Repairs are negotiated, so work to arrive at something acceptable for you both. It's a negotiation, after all, and everyone wants to walk away feeling that they "won."

Backing out of your contract

Yes, it happens. There are many reasons sellers change their mind in the middle of the process. Perhaps a couple who has separated gets back together. Maybe the job transfer fell through. It could even be that the thought of someone else moving into "your" home and changing it is too much to imagine, so you decide to keep it after all.

Can you, the seller, back out? It depends. Up until both you and the buyer have agreed to the terms of

Once both you and the buyer have accepted the terms of the contract and communicated that acceptance to each other, a binding contract exists.

the contract, you can back out because it is not yet binding. Once both you and the buyer have accepted the terms of the contract and communicated that to each other, a binding contract exists. After that, it gets more complicated, but a binding contract can be cancelled.

Some more common examples include:

- **Repairs**—Most offers are contingent upon a limit to what repairs will cost. If repairs are too much for you to pay and you can't negotiate a lower selling price with the prospective buyer, the contract may be cancelled.

- **Specific performance**—If there is a signed, binding contract between you and the buyer and you simply change your mind, the buyer may be able to sue you for "specific performance" and force you to sell. At this point, it may be possible to pay damages to the buyer to release you from the contract.

- **Title search**—The title search may find something that makes the title untransferable and, if it will take months to resolve, the buyer may not have time to wait and may need to move on. This could leave you responsible to reimburse the buyer for expenses already incurred for the purchase such as inspections, mortgage applications, and appraisals.

Always check with your real estate agent, title company or closing attorney to verify your situation.

Time frame?

Once you have an accepted offer and your house is under contract, how long will it take to get to the closing table? Again,

It's not uncommon for closings to take 60 days or more.

patience is in order. It's not uncommon for closings to take 60 days or more. Everyone's backed up: appraisers, underwriters, processors. They have far more accountability than in recent years. Actually, this new process is what it always should have been, more safe and accurate.

The offer is accepted, now what?

Celebration! Almost.
Getting your house ready to market. Done.
Getting an offer. Done.
Negotiating until you have a signed agreement. Done.
Finished? Not quite.
What's left?

Getting the buyer all the way to the closing table

- Step 1 is your buyer getting final approval for a loan. They came to you with a pre-approval letter, but now the price and your home have to be approved.

- Next, your home will be inspected by a professional. They are paid to find what is wrong with the house, and they will. We will discuss home inspections in the next chapter.

- All of the repairs, of course, are part of the ongoing negotiations. The buyer will, more than likely, want everything on the inspection list taken care of by you before closing. Wouldn't you want the same when you are buying a home? So be prepared to spend some time and money getting items repaired that show up on the inspector's list.

- Finally (yes, we're that close), the agent, title company, or closing attorney will schedule a closing which will include a title search to make sure your property is legally owned by you, has no additional liens attached to it, and can be transferred to the new buyer.

Get through all this, and you're ready for the movers.

Chapter 20

HOME INSPECTIONS— WHAT TO LOOK FOR

The buyer will hire, and pay for, a licensed home inspector.

Why does the buyer need an inspection?

Chances are the buyer won't need to request it because most lenders require an inspection before closing. They want to know the condition of the property they are lending against.

A home inspector will check the mechanical, structural, and electrical condition of the structure. He will look for problems and defects, and point out issues and repairs that need attention. His focus includes: roof, siding, plumbing, electrical systems, heating and air units, ventilation, insulation, water heater, pest infiltration, foundation, doors, ceilings, walls, floor, and sometimes your water source and quality.

Home inspectors are paid to find things wrong with the house and they will.

Home inspectors are paid to find things wrong with the house and they will. By crawling under the house and in the attic, they find all kinds of interesting things. It's not uncommon to get a list of repair items five to ten pages long, so don't be surprised. Their interest is the condition of the property, not the outcome of the sale. Inspectors are the buyer's opportunity to protect themselves from potential hidden problems and expense before taking possession of the property.

Most sellers have no idea how much those repairs are going to cost. Especially in today's real estate market, buyers want all these things repaired.

The strangest repair request we ever had was when an inspector pulled down the attic stairs and said they hit the floor at the wrong angle. We had the bottom of those stairs shaved a bit so the angle hit the floor more in line with what pleased the inspector!

Things not covered in a home inspection include:

- Asbestos
- Radon Gas
- Lead Paint
- Toxic Mold
- Pest Control

These items require a specific license to inspect and identify.

Pre-inspection and repairs

It's a good idea to have a pre-inspection before listing your property to know what will be found once you have a contract and the buyer has it inspected. This pre-inspection lets you know what repairs are needed and gives you time to get cost estimates. It also lets you know what items you need to fix before you put the house on the market.

It's best to repair some of the items before your home is sold to speed up the process when you do have your offer in hand. We find it better to do repairs ahead of time rather than making concessions during contract negotiations because concessions on needed repairs or upgrades often cost more than fixing them ahead of time.

Concessions on needed repairs or upgrades often cost more than fixing them ahead of time.

Every inspector will find different problems, so expect more items with your contract. However, with a pre-inspection you are closer to a quick and successful closing when you have your buyer.

Chapter 21

APPRAISAL

n order to sell a property, you, your buyer, and the lender must agree on the value. As we discussed in Chapter 14, Determining Your Property Value, many factors go into determining the fair market value of your home, including what someone is ultimately willing to pay for it. Most lenders require an appraisal, a valuation of the property by an authorized appraiser who is a licensed, independent, non-interested third party.

> *Most lenders require an appraisal, a valuation of the property by an appraiser who is a licensed, independent, non-interested third party.*

Is an appraisal different from a comp?

The quick definition for a comp, or comparable, is a collection of recent sales prices of similar local homes: basically, what houses of the same approximate size in the surrounding area have been selling for.

Though very similar, an appraisal is much more detailed and specific to your property than a comp and is performed by a licensed appraiser. An appraisal is typically required by the buyer's mortgage company to confirm that the value of a home is equal to or higher than the value on the mortgage application.

Why do you need an appraisal

- Most lenders require an appraisal because they don't want to lend more than the actual value of the property.

- Real estate transactions occur very infrequently. This means that property value from sale date to sale date can vary significantly.

- Every property is unique. Properties differ from each other in many ways, including size, condition, structural detail, and location, and this ultimately requires qualified specialists to advise on the value.

Appraisers provide a written report on the value to his or her client. These reports may be used as the basis for mortgage loans. The appraisal can be used by you and/or your real estate agent to set the sale price of the property appraised.

What to do if the appraisal comes out too low

After you and the buyer have reached an agreement and have a signed contract, an appraisal will be performed. There is always the chance that the home will not appraise for as much as the agreed to contract price. In this case, what happens next?

There is always the chance that the home will not appraise for as much as the agreed to contract price.

▧ If the buyer is willing, you can continue on at the agreed upon price. Unless the contract is contingent upon a satisfactory appraisal by either the buyer or the lender, the appraisal is really nothing more than additional information on your property.

▧ The appraisal can be disputed. Perhaps items can be pointed out that were missed and the appraised amount can be raised. Or, if the lender allows, have a second appraiser appraise it.

▧ You can come down on your asking price. Again, it's important to know all of your numbers going into the process so you know immediately if lowering your selling price is an option.

▧ You and the buyer may be able to split the difference to reach a compromise.

▧ You can simply place the property back on the market.

Chapter 22

CLOSING COSTS

losing costs are various fees charged by those involved with the transfer of the property from you, the seller, to the buyer. Some fees are paid by the seller; some are paid by the buyer. Who pays what is always negotiable.

These "closing costs" pay for items such as title policies, recording fees, inspections, courier charges, and fees that lenders charge. The amount of these fees depends largely upon where you live.

Do not ignore closing costs as part of the cost to sell your home.

Closing costs can range from 1 percent to 8 percent, though they are usually 3 percent to 5 percent of the total purchase price. Do not ignore closing costs as part of the cost to sell your home.

What the seller typically pays

- Real estate commission—6 percent of the selling price in most areas

- Loan payoff—to your current lender

- Repairs—found by the buyer's home inspection

- Home warranty—A service contract that covers the repair or replacement of some of the most frequently occurring breakdowns of certain home system components, i.e., heating and air conditioner units, water heater, and appliances. The service contract is good for one year and today's buyers expect this to be provided by the seller.

- Transfer taxes—vary by state, even county

- Attorney fees

- Closing costs—negotiated on behalf of buyer

- Other fees—negotiated during the transaction

- Then there are recording fees, document prep fees, courier fees, etc.

What the buyer typically pays

- All fees to do with obtaining the loan

- Appraisal—to confirm purchase price does not exceed market value

- Home inspection

- Pest inspection—especially in most Southern states because, in humid climates, there are many crawly things that eat and destroy homes (termites, powder post beetles, flying ants, etc.).

- Homeowners insurance—typically prepaid for one year at closing

- Mortgage insurance—if they borrow more than 80 percent of the value of the property

- Survey—often not required, but a wise decision because it does make sure property boundaries and easements are accurate.

- Property taxes—from the day of closing to December 31

- Interest—mortgage interest paid from date of closing through the last day of the month before the first payment is due.

- Attorney fees

- Title insurance

- Escrow fees—if they escrow any taxes or insurance

- Loan discount points—if they paid for a lower interest rate

- Fee for recording the documents.

- Transfer taxes—if there are any. Many states charge a tax to transfer property to a new owner. For example, $1 per $1,000 of selling price. Check with county, not state, to find out your rates.

> *In today's buyer's market, most of the closing costs are paid by the seller.*

A mortgage loan originator or real estate agent can tell you which fees are customarily paid for by the buyer and which by the seller.

Closing costs are one of the things that are negotiable in the purchase contract. In today's buyer's market, most of the costs are paid by the seller.

Closing cost definitions

- Appraisal fee—The lender will require an appraisal. They want to confirm the value of the property they are lending against. The appraisal fee is paid to an appraiser to obtain an estimate of market value of the property.

- Attorney fee—Attorney fees are paid to the closing attorney or title company for closing the transaction.

- Credit report—An evaluation by a credit bureau of the buyer's credit habits.

- Hazard insurance—Insurance that protects a property owner against damage caused by fires, severe storms, earthquakes, or other natural events. Typically, the buyer will be required to pay for a year's worth of premiums at closing, but this will depend on the exact details of the policy.

- Inspection fees—Lenders require a general property inspection before they will lend on a property. There will also be a fee for any additional inspections the buyer wants done, including: septic inspection, termite and pest inspections, mold, radon gas, etc.

- Loan origination fee—A lender's fee to the borrower for establishing a new loan. Conventional loan origination fees range from one to three points. A point is equal to one percent of the loan. For example, on a $100,000 home, a point is $1,000.

- Mortgage insurance—Typically required on conventional loans when borrowing more than 80 percent of the appraised value. The cost may range from one half percent to 1 percent per year and fourteen months' premium is often collected at closing. This is coverage for the lender in case the borrower defaults.

- Prepaid interest—Mortgage interest from the date of closing through the last day of the month before the first payment is due.

- Recording fees—Charges by the county recorder to record documents required to clear or transfer title.

- Survey—Shows boundaries of a piece of real estate, whether buildings or other improvements are actually located on the property, and that surrounding buildings, utilities, or improvements do not encroach on the property.

- Tax and insurance escrow—If the new loan is going to have an escrow account for the payment of taxes and insurance, the lender will require payments to be deposited at the time of closing, depending upon when the next taxes or insurance need to be paid out of the escrow account.

- Title examination fee—Cost to review the title to the property for liens, mortgages, easements, or defects.

- Title insurance—Covers title defects and certain unrecorded liens that may not be found in the title examination. Cost of title insurance is based on the loan amount or purchase price and is required by most lenders. The cost depends on the amount of the loan for a lender's policy, or the purchase price for an owner's policy. A lender's title insurance policy is paid for by the buyer but does not insure the buyer but the lender.

HUD-1 Settlement Statement

Confusion regarding the HUD-1 is common, so let me simplify:

Anytime you buy or sell a piece of real estate, you receive, at or before closing, a summary of all fees associated with the purchase or sale on a document called a HUD-1 Settlement Statement. This form will be filled out by the closing attorney or title company and will be displayed to both you and the buyer at closing to show all fees each of you will pay to purchase, transfer, and record the transfer of property.

Always ask that a copy of the HUD-1 Settlement Statement be provided to you twenty-four hours before your scheduled closing so you can confirm all fees you are to pay and the amount you will receive or, perhaps, need to bring to closing. This is common practice but often does not happen unless there is a specific request for it to the attorney or closing agent.

When you receive the HUD-1, examine it closely to find errors or omissions. Never assume it was prepared correctly. We regularly find mistakes on the HUD-1. If you find errors, have them corrected. And, if there are items you don't understand, ask questions until you do.

The HUD-1 is a three page document and is broken down into easily understood sections (see insert). The top area is self-explanatory with sections for buyer, seller, lender, and property information. The sections below are broken into two columns, the left includes a summary of the buyer's/borrower's transaction; the right column is for the seller's.

Read your column and you will find it broken into transactional groups including: gross amount due (to or from you), loan payoff, commission to be paid, taxes, attorney fees, recording fees, etc.

Any items associated with the purchase or sale, but paid either before or after closing, should also show up on the HUD-1. These items will be marked with the letters "POC," meaning Paid Outside of Closing. They are included on the HUD-1 because this form is intended to be a record of all costs associated with the property transfer.

As with any legal document, when looked at as a whole, it can seem overwhelming. When you sit down and read it in sections, it is actually quite easy to understand.

Again, if you find something you don't understand, ask questions until you do. The closing attorney/ closing agent, real estate agent, and/or lender are all there on your behalf and expect to answer questions for buyers and sellers everyday.

Always ask that a copy of the HUD-1 be provided to you twenty-four hours before closing so you can confirm all fees you are to pay and the amount you will receive or, perhaps, need to bring to closing.

OMB Approval No. 2502-0265

A. **Settlement Statement (HUD-1)**

B. Type of Loan					
1. ☐ FHA 2. ☐ RHS 3. ☐ Conv. Unins. 4. ☐ VA 5. ☐ Conv. Ins.		6. File Number:	7. Loan Number:	8. Mortgage Insurance Case Number:	

C. Note: This form is furnished to give you a statement of actual settlement costs. Amounts paid to and by the settlement agent are shown. Items marked "(p.o.c.)" were paid outside the closing; they are shown here for informational purposes and are not included in the totals.

D. Name & Address of Borrower:	E. Name & Address of Seller:	F. Name & Address of Lender:
G. Property Location:	H. Settlement Agent: Place of Settlement:	I. Settlement Date:

J. Summary of Borrower's Transaction		K. Summary of Seller's Transaction	
100. Gross Amount Due from Borrower		**400. Gross Amount Due to Seller**	
101. Contract sales price		401. Contract sales price	
102. Personal property		402. Personal property	
103. Settlement charges to borrower (line 1400)		403.	
104.		404.	
105.		405.	
Adjustment for items paid by seller in advance		Adjustment for items paid by seller in advance	
106. City/town taxes to		406. City/town taxes to	
107. County taxes to		407. County taxes to	
108. Assessments to		408. Assessments to	
109.		409.	
110.		410.	
111.		411.	
112.		412.	
120. Gross Amount Due from Borrower		**420. Gross Amount Due to Seller**	
200. Amount Paid by or in Behalf of Borrower		**500. Reductions In Amount Due to seller**	
201. Deposit or earnest money		501. Excess deposit (see instructions)	
202. Principal amount of new loan(s)		502. Settlement charges to seller (line 1400)	
203. Existing loan(s) taken subject to		503. Existing loan(s) taken subject to	
204.		504. Payoff of first mortgage loan	
205.		505. Payoff of second mortgage loan	
206.		506.	
207.		507.	
208.		508.	
209.		509.	
Adjustments for items unpaid by seller		Adjustments for items unpaid by seller	
210. City/town taxes to		510. City/town taxes to	
211. County taxes to		511. County taxes to	
212. Assessments to		512. Assessments to	
213.		513.	
214.		514.	
215.		515.	
216.		516.	
217.		517.	
218.		518.	
219.		519.	
220. Total Paid by/for Borrower		**520. Total Reduction Amount Due Seller**	
300. Cash at Settlement from/to Borrower		**600. Cash at Settlement to/from Seller**	
301. Gross amount due from borrower (line 120)		601. Gross amount due to seller (line 420)	
302. Less amounts paid by/for borrower (line 220)	( )	602. Less reductions in amounts due seller (line 520)	( )
303. Cash ☐ From ☐ To Borrower		**603. Cash** ☐ To ☐ From Seller	

The Public Reporting Burden for this collection of information is estimated at 35 minutes per response for collecting, reviewing, and reporting the data. This agency may not collect this information, and you are not required to complete this form, unless it displays a currently valid OMB control number. No confidentiality is assured; this disclosure is mandatory. This is designed to provide the parties to a RESPA covered transaction with information during the settlement process.

A final walk through

Your buyer may request a final walk through the property the day of closing, before you close. It is important for them to check the condition of the property one more time to make sure everything agreed to is still there: light fixtures, window treatments, appliances, etc.

Make sure nothing was damaged between the time the inspector looked at it and the day of closing. Homes can be damaged during the move-out process and vacant homes may have been vandalized. Confirm what you are selling before the day of closing.

After the final walk through, the buyer should sign a release stating that the walk through was done and they accept the property in its current condition. This protects you from claims they may try to bring against you after your settlement date.

Section 6

SOLD!

At last, success!

In this section, I'll cover what happens the day of closing and how the property is legally transferred from you to the buyer.

Next, helpful tips to make your move go as smoothly and swiftly as possible.

I wrap up with the risks of leaving your home vacant and, the bonus section, how to protect your home from burglaries.

You've accomplished your biggest task, getting your home sold. Congratulations! Now let's look forward to the next step.

Chapter 23

THE CLOSING

Y ou've made it. You prepared, marketed, negotiated, and sold your home. The day of closing, both you and the buyer show up at the agreed location to sign documents that will transfer the property ownership from seller to buyer.

It's an exciting day. What should you expect?

Where does the closing take place?

Depending upon your state regulations, closing will most likely occur at the office of an attorney or a title company.

Who attends the closing?

Typically, the seller, the buyer, and the closing agent (attorney or title company representative) will all be present together at the closing. Often, the real estate agent for both the buyers and the sellers also attend. The agents are there to help handle any discrepancies that may come up at the last minute.

It is absolutely possible and acceptable for the buyers and sellers to show up at different times. The important thing is to get all documentation signed on the same day in order to have everything recorded, funds distributed, and the ownership transferred.

It is not required, however, for both buyers and sellers to show up at the same time.

What happens at the closing?

Everyone is seated together at a conference table. The closing agent will go over the HUD-1 Settlement Statement (discussed in Chapter 22– Closing Costs) to make sure everyone understands and agrees to all costs as printed on the document. Once the document is approved as printed, everyone signs and receives an original, signed copy for their closing packet.

Typically, the closing agent will go over the seller's side of the HUD-1 first and have the seller agree and sign. At that time, the seller is free to leave, or stay, while the buyer goes over their part of the details next.

Once all documents are recorded and funds are disbursed, the transfer of ownership is complete.

After the buyer completes their part of the process, they may leave as well. At that time, the closing agent is responsible to record the documents and transfer any necessary funds to and/or from both buyer and seller. Once all documents are recorded and funds are disbursed, the transfer of ownership is complete.

Chapter 24

THE MOVING PROCESS AND TIPS

Finally, you're home is sold so you'll be moving. Be prepared, be organized, and have fun! The last time I moved, we had been in the house for eleven years and our two children had moved out—without all their stuff! We had A LOT to move!

Cleaning up and clearing out

Heads up: when you know you are going to move, join a gym. The amount of physical work you are about to experience cannot be over emphasized! Getting fit will actually help avoid injuries and exhaustion.

So, what's first in the moving process? As soon as you decide to list your property, start cleaning it out. You can never clean out too soon, too often, or too much. The best feng shui advice is GET RID OF THE CLUTTER!

If you are not using something, pass it on. Start the cleaning out process with your shoes and clothes. When the clothes are nice enough for someone else to use, but things you no longer wear, pass them on.

Then there are the unnecessary knick-knacks. Pack those up to give away. Cleaning out the closets and drawers is therapeutic. It feels good and increases the energy in your home to get rid of the excess, and to know you are helping someone else who can use what you do not.

Planning a yard sale? I found this great website: YardSaleTreasureMap.com. The site allows you to put in your address, the distance you want to drive, and the day you plan to shop. Apparently, the list comes from sales posted on Craigslist. com so, if you plan to sell, be sure your information is posted there so shoppers can find you.

Cleaning up, clearing out, and getting rid of ALL clutter will really help sell your home.

Cleaning up, clearing out, and getting rid of ALL clutter will really help sell your home. You want to make your home look as spacious as possible to the next owner, so get rid of anything you don't need or use now.

Packing tips

Sometimes, a closing can happen sooner than expected. It's always possible that a cash buyer will show up and be able to close in only two weeks. Be prepared!

Start saving newspapers. Ask friends and neighbors to save theirs for you. You can never have too much packing material. Buy bubble wrap for dishes, glasses, and breakables. Consider using green packing materials and moving companies, which you can find online.

Grocery stores and liquor stores are great sources for strong boxes (for free!). Most stores crush their boxes after emptying so ask them to save boxes for you. Sometimes they have boxes available, or they may be willing to collect them and tell you when to come back to pick them up.

Do not use paper or plastic bags. Items are not protected, and bags tear and spill. Having everything in boxes makes it easy to stack and pack in the moving truck.

Cheap paper towels work nicely as packing material since they are clean (no newsprint to transfer), come on a roll so they can be sized appropriately, and can be used for cleaning after you unpack. Old clothes or linens that you

It's always possible that a cash buyer will show up and be able to close in only two weeks. Be prepared!

plan to donate or throw away also make great packing material.

When packing, use different colored boxes for different rooms. Or, use different colored tape or stickers so you or the movers know which room to take each box in your new home. Clearly mark all boxes. That way, when you get to the new home, you will know where the boxes go, what you want to open first, and what can wait until later or go into storage.

When taping boxes, be sure to use packing tape. It is the only kind that will really hold through the trials of moving. Duct tape does not stick well to cardboard and may break lose. Whatever tape you use, get twice as much as you think you'll need and you'll probably still run out.

Clothes are okay to leave in drawers during transport, but everything else should be taken out and boxed for safety and ease of movement. Take out all valuables, such as jewelry, and anything breakable or heavy.

Always clearly mark the FRAGILE items. Lamps, china, computers, stereos, and DVD players must all be carefully packed and marked for safety. Remember how well they were packed when you bought them?

Wardrobe boxes are a worthwhile investment. Simply take the clothes out of your closets and hang them on the hanging bar in the box. No folding necessary. These boxes save a ton of time and energy. Storage facilities often sell wardrobe boxes and unusually sized boxes for those awkwardly shaped items.

If you are moving appliances, be sure to empty the contents of the refrigerator and freezer. Take everything out of the oven and drawers. All appliances must be empty, drawers and doors secured so they don't fly open during transport.

Scheduling

As soon as you know your moving date, choose a moving company and make a reservation. Especially May through August, available trucks can be hard to find. Ask the moving scheduler what requirements they have for packing your belongings, and don't underestimate how much stuff you have and how much it weighs. The last thing you need is for the movers to show up, only to refuse to load your stuff until they've repacked it, or not load it all because there's not enough room on their truck.

Check and recheck all appointments. When you're packed and ready to go, the movers not showing on time, the cable guy not coming as scheduled, the power company forgetting to send someone to read the meter so they can turn off and/or transfer your electrical, all of these and many other things can really mess up your move. Re-confirm appointments! Make sure the person you talked with really scheduled your appointment. It takes some time, but the mistake you prevent will be well worth it.

And, finally

Things happen. Not everything goes as planned, so expect that when you start out. Be well rested and have food throughout the moving day. If possible, have a friend bring dinner over while everyone is unpacking. There is nothing better than sitting down to a wonderful meal when your body is ready to collapse!

There will be repair issues in the new home that you did not expect, so expect them. This is all part of the experience of the new place. You will want to change things to make the house yours. Give yourself time, do it with love, enjoy every minute of your new adventure and . . . Welcome Home!

Chapter 25

RISKS OF LEAVING YOUR HOME VACANT

A typical homeowner's insurance policy ends once the property has been vacant for thirty days. Most homeowners continue to pay their premium but, if a claim is filed, it may not be paid because vacancy voids the policy.

If you leave a home vacant, you must have vacancy insurance. Premiums for this type of insurance can be more than double regular insurance.

Insurance companies put a high risk (and cost) on insuring vacant homes because of the increased risk of theft, vandalism, fire, and water damage. These risks and costs may be higher in Northern states because of potential damage due to extreme

> *A typical homeowner's insurance policy ends once the property has been vacant for thirty days.*

weather (frozen pipes bursting, etc.). Ask your agent about vacancy insurance.

Not all insurance companies insure vacant houses, so check around. If your company does not, look online for an insurance company that does.

It may be cheaper, and safer, to keep your "for sale" home occupied. Before you move out, take a look at your policy and talk with your insurance agent for guidance.

Some suggestions when thinking about vacating your property:

- Protect your property. Install and use a monitored home security system.

- Make sure the smoke detectors are functioning.

- Vacant or not, if your home has a sprinkler system, monitored central alarm for fire, smoke and theft, and deadbolt locks, your home is safer and these features can lower your insurance premiums so notify your agent.

- Make the house look lived-in. Have someone bring in mail. It's always better to stop mail and other deliveries any time you're away. Ask a neighbor to park his or her car in your driveway. Install timers on lights and leave window coverings and some furniture in the home.

- If possible, don't move out until you've sold the home. Perhaps someone in the family can stay behind or live there occasionally until the home is sold.

- Rent out the home. Not only will the home be lived in but the rent will help cover your carrying costs. In this case, you will need to change your homeowner's insurance policy to a landlord policy but that will be cheaper than vacant home insurance.

- Hire a house-sitter or let someone you trust live there until it's sold.

- No matter what you do, keep the home maintained by cleaning the yard and gutters, trimming trees, checking for leaks, shoveling sidewalks and driveway, and winterizing or maintaining as necessary.

Whatever you decide, leave the property protected before moving on.

Bonus Section

26 WAYS TO PROTECT YOUR HOME FROM BURGLARIES

E very 14.6 seconds, a home is robbed. Most robberies happen during the day. According to statistics by the Federal Bureau of Investigation, the average dollar loss per burglary is more than $2,000.

It doesn't take much to get the thieves to leave your house alone.

With the current economy, burglary is on the rise. Good news, it doesn't take much to get thieves to leave your house alone. What can you do to keep your home secure?

1. **Have a secure front door**—The front door is the No. 1 point of entry for thieves. Most of the time, they knock to see if you're home, then just stand back and kick in the front door. Make sure it's an exterior door, different than what you'd use

for the bedroom. Make sure it's solid core construction or metal clad. And make sure it's secured by 3" screws rather than the typical 1" so it's secured to the structure, rather than just the door frame.

2. **Peep hole**—Have one in your door so it doesn't have to be opened to see who's there. The best ones are wide-angle viewers.

3. **Exterior doors**—Sixty percent of all burglaries take place at ground floor doors and windows. All entry doors should be solid wood or steel-wrapped wood-core doors.

4. **Garage doors and windows**—Should be treated as any exterior door and window. Keep them closed and locked. Burglars can enter through your garage undetected from the outside. Once inside the garage, a burglar can use your tools to break into your home, out of sight of the neighbors.

5. **Porch and patio doors**—Take extra precaution because these doors are less observable from the street and by neighbors.

6. **Locks**—Key-in-the-knob locks can be forced quickly and without much effort. If you have this type of lock, be sure to add a dead bolt. And, not all dead bolts are the same. Research to get one that will truly secure your door. Be sure to attach the dead bolt with three-inch screws that penetrate through the frame to the structure. If you have glass within 40 inches of the dead bolt, it is recommended that you use a dead bolt lock that is key operated from both inside and out. (Don't leave the key sitting in the inside lock or, by simply breaking the glass, someone can reach in and unlock the door!)

7. **Windows**—All ground floor windows should be closed and locked when you're away. Keep bushes and shrubs trimmed back so your windows are not hidden, which would give privacy to intruders. And make sure all tree branches are

cut back from upper level windows to prevent access. Close and lock upper floor windows when you are away.

8. **Basement windows**—Keep closed and locked. If not used, secure permanently with nails that extend into the structure.

9. **Lock windows and doors**—Having secured doors and windows is not enough. They must be locked! I was surprised to read that many people don't bother. Of all reported burglaries, 33.2 percent were unlawful entries (without force)—meaning the house wasn't even locked.

10. **Close shades and curtains in the evening**—One way thieves decide where to strike is simply by window-shopping. Close the blinds so they won't see what you have.

11. **Spare keys**—Don't hide spare keys. Burglars know about fake rocks and statues and will check under doormats, in mailboxes, and over doorways. Make sure everyone in the family has a spare key and give a spare set to a neighbor.

12. **Ladders**—Don't store ladders outdoors or in unlocked sheds. These can be used to reach the roof and upper floor windows.

13. **Silent alarms**—We all hate noisy alarms, so do burglars. Smart thieves know it can take 10 to 20 minutes for the alarm company or police to show up after an alarm has been tripped. It's best to have both silent and audible alarms.

14. **Landscaping**—Tall hedges and shrubs near the house create hiding spots. Keep doorways, porches and windows clear. Overhanging branches can be a way to access upper decks or your roof.

15. **Lawn Care**—A well-manicured lawn indicates someone is home. Be sure to have your lawn cared for even when on vacation or if you move and leave the home vacant.

16. **Exterior lighting**—All exterior entrances should be well lighted. Poor lighting allows dark and shadows where burglars can work unobserved. Many can be controlled to go on and off depending upon daylight and motion sensors go on automatically in response to motion. This sudden light not only scares away intruders but alerts you and your neighbors as well.

17. **Indoor timers**—When away from home, leave a few lights on. Use timers to turn lights on and off at normal times. You can even set TVs or radios to turn on and off. Set timers to go on thirty minutes before dark so it looks like someone is in the house. While on vacation, have them go off at random times when you'd normally go to bed.

18. **Sliding glass doors**—Most are easy to jiggle free of locks and slide open easily. An inexpensive security measure is to place a dowel in the channel so the door can't be pried open. Sliding doors are lifted into position when installed and can be lifted from the track to be removed by a burglar. Insert two or three sheet metal screws into the track above the door to prevent this. Adjust the screws so the top of the door barely clears them when opened or closed. Lock the door with a dead bolt.

19. **Install deadbolts**—Especially on a door with a glass section or located near a window. With a deadbolt, if the glass is broken and someone tries to reach in to open the door, they won't be able to. There are two main types of deadbolts: single and double cylinder locks. A single cylinder deadbolt has a keyed opening on one side and a knob that can be turned by hand on the other. A double cylinder deadbolt lock is keyed on both sides.

20. **Don't rely on your dog barking dog**—Serious burglars know dogs may back away from someone with a weapon, or happily accept a treat laced with a tranquilizer. Better to make your home look occupied with timers that turn electronics on and off in random patterns.

21. **Watch what you throw out**—Don't advertise your brand-new flat-screen TV, computer, or other big-ticket item by putting boxes at the curb with your trash. Break down boxes into small pieces and bundle them so you can't tell what was inside.

22. **Social media**—Never post vacation info on Facebook or any other social media sites. Burglars troll social media sites looking for targets. Wait until you get back before sharing vacation details.

23. **GPS**—NEVER use your home address in your GPS. Thieves break into cars, and then steal the GPS and garage door opener. Now they know where you live and have the ability to break in. Instead use a location, preferably a business, near you as your home location.

24. **Mail, newspapers, and FedEx**—When out of town, be sure to stop your mail, newspapers, and any other scheduled deliveries. At the very least, have a neighbor pick them up for you daily. Nothing says, "we're not here" like deliveries piling up at your home.

25. **Don't hesitate!**—Report suspicious activities in your neighborhood. I once had two men knock on my door. One was holding a clipboard. They claimed to be from the local electric company and said they needed to see my last three electric bills. I said that I didn't have them, that they'd need to send the request by mail, and I shut the door. I ran to the phone and called the electric company. Of course, they would never do such a thing. So I phoned the police and every neighbor whose phone number I had.

Which brings me to the final suggestion.

26. **Neighborhood Watch program**—How about forming one in your neighborhood? The neighbors learn how to secure their homes, agree to report suspicious activities on their block, have a communication network established, and put

out signs to alert intruders driving through the area. Again, anyone interested in committing a crime will move on to another area.

It's easy and inexpensive to minimize your chance of being a target. Simply make forced entry difficult or risky and any burglar will move onto another property. Your local law enforcement will be happy to advise and assist you and your neighbors.

Crime prevention begins at home!

Epilogue

I have been investing in real estate since 2004, and I now do coaching and training for real estate investors (check out our website: www.TriadMastermind.com). I write real estate articles for my blog four to five times per week at www.KarensPerspective.com, and I write books.

What I've found when directing buyers, sellers, and investors to my website is that many of you prefer to hold the printed word rather than read a blog. You want to mark it up, make notes in the margin, and tag pages for reference.

For you, I've put together my books taken, in large part, from my blog posts. I've elaborated them in printed form so you have all the information you need to carry with you and reference with ease.

Many thanks to you for your interest, and if you are left with unanswered questions or have a real estate story or success you'd like to share, contact me on my blog www.KarensPerspective.com/contact or email me at karen@karensperspective.com.

I look forward to hearing from you and may you have tremendous real estate success!

About the Author

 Karen Rittenhouse is a full-time real estate investor. She's been involved in real estate since 2000, when she purchased her first investment property, and full-time since January 2005. In the past few years, Karen has bought and sold more than 150 single-family homes. She is not a real estate agent. All of the deals with which she's been involved have been her own.

Karen also does local coaching and training, and has found through her travels nationally that many people recognize the value of investing in real estate—some with only their personal homes, others as a way to produce present and future income. Most people simply don't know how to get started, what to do next, or where to get information. That's the purpose of her writing—concise, abundant information.

Before turning to real estate, Karen sold high-end furniture and did interior design. So, as you can see, much of her working career has been involved with creating nurturing home environments. Her goal here is to help people on their path to real estate success.

To share much needed information, Karen writes books and blogs about real estate at www.KarensPerspective.com. Be sure to check out her book for buyers, The Essential Handbook for Buying a Home.

For questions or comments, you can reach her at karen@karensperspective.com.

Terms & Definitions

For ease of use, following is an alphabetical listing of terms used in this book. They aren't all official definitions; many are friendly explanations as I would explain them in person. For more real estate definitions, check out one of my favorite sites, Investopedia.com.

Absolute Auction—The winning bid purchases the property. There is no minimum bid amount and no need for lender confirmation.

Adjustable Rate Mortgage (ARM)—Mortgage where the interest rate paid on the outstanding balance varies over time. The initial interest rate starts low for a period of time and increases periodically, in some cases, every month.

Balloon Payment—Oversize payment due at the end of a mortgage. The entire loan amount is not amortized over the life of the loan, but the remaining balance is due as a final repayment.

Capital Gains—Profits a seller realizes when he or she sells the capital asset (property) for a price higher than the purchase price.

Capital Gains Tax—A tax levied on the profits a seller realizes when he or she sells the capital asset (property).

Closing—Finalizing the sale! Time when all documents are signed and recorded. This is the time when the ownership of the property is transferred from seller to buyer.

Comparable Sale—Comp—Sales of similar homes in the same or similar neighborhood as the property you are evaluating. By comparing similar characteristics between homes of comparable size, value, and age, a buyer is better able to determine the true property value of the home they want to purchase.

Closing Costs—Costs over and above the price of the property, all to do with the transfer of the property. Costs include a variety of things like loan origination fees, discount points, appraisal fees, title searches, title insurance, surveys, taxes, deed-recording fees, and credit report charges. These costs are typically paid at the closing.

Commission—A charge for providing services.

Contingency—A provision for an event or circumstance that may, but is not certain, to occur.

Counter Offer—An offer made in response to an unacceptable offer. A counter is a new offer and starts the offer process over. A counter offer is a way to decline a previous offer while allowing negotiations to continue.

Credit Report—Evaluation by a credit bureau of the buyer's credit habits.

Credit Score—A numeric expression of your creditworthiness ranging from 350 to 800.

Debt to income ratio—how much debt you have compared with how much pre-tax income you bring in to cover that debt.

Default—Failure to make a payment when due.

Deficiency Judgment—Occurs when the lender does not release the borrower from a personal obligation to repay the full amount that was owed before a short sale occurred. In this instance, the borrower remains liable for the full amount of the remaining loan balance even if the property is sold for less.

Discount Points—Prepaid interest you can purchase to lower the interest you will be paying monthly. The discount points you buy actually pay the lender interest today rather than over time. Each discount point generally costs 1 percent of your loan amount and lowers your interest rate by one-eighth percent to one one-quarter percent.

Due Diligence—Thorough investigation before entering into a contract or agreement.

Due on Sale Clause—In a mortgage contract, requires the mortgage to be immediately paid in full if the property is sold or transferred to a new owner.

Earnest Money Deposit—Money submitted with purchase and sale agreement to show seller that buyer is serious about purchasing a property. At closing, the deposit is credited toward the buyer's down payment.

Easement—A right to use the real property of another without possessing it. For example, utility companies have easements giving them the right to run utility pipes and lines underground through your property. Watch out when digging!

Equity—The difference between what is owed on the mortgage and what the property is worth.

Escrow—Monies held by a third party on behalf of lender and borrower. When all agreement conditions are met, the money held in escrow transfers to the appropriate entities. For example, property taxes or mortgage insurance is often "held in escrow" out of every monthly payment until they are due. When the tax or mortgage insurance payment is due, those monies are transferred from your escrow account and sent to pay your tax or mortgage insurance. Most mortgage lenders are not willing to risk that a homeowner will not pay property tax or insurance, so they require these monies to be escrowed.

Fair Market Value—The price a given property would sell for.

FHA Loan—Mortgage issued by federally qualified lenders and insured by the Federal Housing Administration (FHA). FHA loans are designed for low-to-moderate-income borrowers who are unable to make a large down payment. FHA loans are popular with first-time buyers because they are able to borrow up to 97 percent of the value of the home. The 3 percent down payment can come from a gift or a grant.

Financing—Providing funds for a purchase.

Fixed Interest Rate—An interest rate that will not change.

Fixture—Physical property that is permanently attached or fixed to the home, which, if removed, would cause damage. An example would be a ceiling fan, light fixture, or attached drapery rods.

Flat Fee Listing—When a company or agent puts your property on the MLS, charging you a fee to do this. There is no commission associated with a flat fee listing.

Foreclosure—Termination of the mortgage rights of the home-owner. Taking possession of a mortgaged property because someone failed to make his or her mortgage payments.

FSBO—For Sale by Owner

HOA—Homeowners Association—an organization that assists with maintaining and improving groups of property.

HOA Fees—Money paid monthly by owners of residential property to the Homeowners Association that assists with maintaining and improving that property and others in the same group.

Home Warranty—One-year service contract covering repair or replacement of breakdowns of certain home system components and appliances.

Housing Bubble—Economic bubble that has rapid increases in property values until they reach unsustainable levels until, at that point, they sharply decline.

HUD-1—Form used by closing agent to itemize services and fees imposed on both borrower and seller in a real estate transaction. This form provides each party, at or before closing, with a complete list of incoming and outgoing funds.

HVAC—The home's heating and air conditioning system. Literally, heating, ventilation, and air conditioning.

Junior Lien—Newer loans, loans that come after the primary mortgage note, which is typically the senior lien. Whether a loan is "junior" or "senior" only matters as far as order of payoff if the borrower defaults on their loans. The senior loan is paid off with sales proceeds first; all junior liens are then paid in their order of age—the oldest junior lien paid first.

Lessee—The person or entity leasing property as a tenant.

Lien—Process by which a lender, contractor, or anyone not having unpaid balances due according to the terms of a contract, may place the burden of the unpaid debt upon the property.

Loan Modification—**Loan mod**—a permanent change in one or more of the terms of a loan.

Loan to Value—**LTV**—The loan amount compared to the property value. Indicates the amount of equity in the home.

Market Value—The price for which a given property would sell.

Material Defect—Any defect, tangible or intangible, in a specific property that could affect a buyer's decision to purchase it or affect the property's value (i.e., a cracked foundation).

Mechanics Lien—Because of non-payment, builders, contractors, subcontractors, suppliers of materials, or tradesmen who build or repair the structure may place a lien against the property for any work done or materials used on the property. The lien ensures that they will be paid in the event of sale of the property. A mechanics lien is a junior lien and will be paid in order after the senior lien holder.

MLS—Multiple Listing Service—Where real estate agents publish their property listings.

Mortgage—Debt secured by a piece of real estate. Borrower is obligated to pay back the debt with a predetermined number of payments. Also known as a "lien" against the property.

Mortgage Insurance—Protects lender or titleholder against losses if the borrower defaults on payments, dies, or is unable to meet the obligations of the mortgage. Mortgage insurance is required for borrowers making a down payment of less than 20 percent.

Owner Financing—Or **Seller Financing**—the prospective buyer obtains financing from the owner or seller of the property rather than through a conventional mortgage lender.

Personal Property—Assets other than real estate. In real estate, unlike the land and the building, personal property is movable. Examples are vehicles, furniture, and appliances.

Points—One percent of the amount of the loan.

Prepayment Penalty—Mortgage clause stating that, if the mortgage is paid off early or refinanced within a certain time period, a penalty will be charged. The penalty is typically a percentage of the mortgage balance or a specific number of months worth of interest.

Promissory Note—A binding instrument, where the issuer makes a written promise to pay a determined sum of money to the payee. Under what specific terms the note amount is paid is negotiable, but specifically spelled out in the note.

Purchase Contract—The agreement signed between buyer and seller

Quitclaim Deed—Releases a person's interest in a property but provides no warranties of ownership. A quitclaim deed does not guarantee that the grantor's claim is valid, but it does prevent the grantor from later claiming they have an interest in the property. For example, I can quitclaim my rights to the local country club to you even though I do not have any ownership in the country club. I may get rid of a property this way, but I would certainly never buy one with a quitclaim deed.

REO—Real Estate Owned—Properties banks own because they have taken them back from borrowers who have defaulted on their mortgages.

Second Lien—In real estate, if a second mortgage is taken out on the same property, the second loan is the second lien debt, subordinate to the first mortgage. In case of default, the second lien is paid with proceeds left from the sale after the first lien is paid. For this reason, a second lien is considered riskier than a first, so often comes with a higher interest rate.

Sell with Reserve— At auction, a minimum price is set and must be met before a sale is final

Seller Concessions—Any negotiation where the seller gives something up to the b uyer. Often, a specific dollar amount or percentage of the purchase price that a seller agrees to contribute toward closing costs.

Seller Financing—Or owner financing—the prospective buyer obtains financing from the seller or owner of the property rather than through a conventional mortgage lender.

Short, Shorted, Short Sale—In real estate, when a property is sold "short" of what is owed, the lender agrees to accept less than the full amount of the loan balance as complete repayment of the loan.

Specific Performance—Compels the party to execute a contract according to the terms agreed upon. Grants the suing party what they actually bargained for in the contract rather than damages.

Subject-to—A method of transferring property ownership where the seller deeds the property to a buyer "subject-to" the existing loan, allowing the investor/buyer to pay it off at a later date. The buyer is then on public record as the property owner while the loan stays in the seller's name.

Taking Title—Transferring legal ownership from the seller to the new owner. After transfer, the new owner's name shows on the recorded title, or deed, to the property.

Title—Recognition of ownership

Title Insurance—Covers the loss of a property due to legal defects. Required on any property with a mortgage. Most title insurance is paid for by the borrower but protects only the lender.

Title Search—Examination of public records to confirm property's legal ownership and to discover what claims are filed against the property. Searches check ownership, liens, judgments, loans, and property taxes due on the property.

Wrap Around Loan—Used on a property with an outstanding loan balance. The seller lends the buyer the difference between the existing loan and the purchase price.

Internet Resource Links

Auctions

- EBay Home Auctions
- National Auctioneers Association

Calculators

- **Buying vs. Renting Calculator**
  tinyurl.com/shouldirent
- **Accelerated Mortgage Payoff**
  tinyurl.com/mortpayoff
- **Estate Tax Calculator**
  http://tinyurl.com/estatetaxcalculator

Credit

- FreeCreditReport.com
- AnnualCreditReport.com
- Equifax.com
- Experian.com
- TransUnion.com
- MyFICO.com

Crime Check

- CrimeReports.com
- Crimemapping.com
- Spotcrime.net

Foreclosure Info

- **Foreclosure Laws—State by State**
  tinyurl.com/foreclosurelaws
- **Foreclosure Map—State by State**
  tinyurl.com/foreclosuresbystate
- **Nationwide Foreclosure List**
  foreclosure.com

Free Sites to List Properties

- **Trulia**
  trulia.com
- **Zillow**
  zillow.com
- **Craigslist**
  craigslist.org
- ForSaleByOwner.com
- Postlets.com

Home Values Comparables

- **Home Values Price Check**
  realestate.com/homepricecheck/
- **Real Estate Values Free Comps**
  realestateabc.com/home-values/
- **Eppraisal**
  eppraisal.com/

▦ **Cost of Living Comparisons**
tinyurl.com/areacomparisons

Maps

▦ **Bing**
Bing.com/maps

▦ **Yahoo**
maps.yahoo.com

▦ **Google**
maps.google.com

Additional

▦ **Housing Predictor—forecasts for all 50 states**
housingpredictor.com/

▦ **National Association of Realtors website**
Realtor.org

▦ **Freddie Mac & Fannie Mae mortgages**
government-mortgages.com/

▦ **VA loans**
homeloans.va.gov

▦ **Real Estate Definitions**
Investopedia.com

▦ **Federal Consumer Protection Agency**
ftc.gov/

▦ **Home Inspectors Directory Inspection checklist**
tinyurl.com/inspectionlist

▦ **HUD**
hud.gov

▦ **Sale of Residence—Real Estate Tax Tips**
http://tinyurl.com/retaxtips

Now that You're Ready to Move...

The Essential
Handbook
FOR **BUYING**
A **HOME**

Karen Rittenhouse

**Look for Karen's companion books at
KarensPerspective.com, Amazon.com or
wherever fine books are sold!**

**For more free real estate
information and training,
scan this code or go to
KarenRittenhouseBook.com**

CPSIA information can be obtained
at www.ICGtesting.com
Printed in the USA
BVHW041130230222
629879BV00006B/141

9 780983 775201